# COMPELLING CONVERSATIONS
## 11 Selected Chapters on Timeless Topics
## for the Language Company Students
## Level 2

Written, Compiled, and Edited by
Eric H. Roth and Toni Aberson

Project Director
Wende Weber, Director
The Language Company – Berkeley
Visiting Scholars and Postdoctoral Affairs program

The Language Company – Level 2

Originally Published by:
Chimayo Press

Compelling Conversations
Questions & Quotations on Timeless Topics
An Engaging ESL Textbook for Advanced Students
Copyright © 2008 by Eric H. Roth and Toni Aberson

Additional worksheets ©2011
This special edition copyrighted ©2011

ISBN: 978-09826178-4-7

Library of Congress Reg. # TX 6-377-924

Cover images from The Language Company
Interior photographs by Laurie Selik and iStockphoto.com

**Chimayo Press**
3766 Redwood Ave.
Los Angeles, California
90066-3506
(310) 390-0131
Eric @CompellingConversations.com
www.CompellingConversations.com

Printed in the U.S.A.

**Dedicated to**
**Dani Herbert Joseph Roth**
(1937—1997)

A global citizen, he could talk with almost anyone, in six different languages, and share a laugh. This book attempts to capture some of his generous spirit, wit, and curiosity.

"Own only what you can always carry with you: know languages, know countries, know people. Let your memory be your travel bag."

—Alexander Solzhenitsyn (1918-2008), Russian writer and historian

"One cannot always be a hero, but one can always be human."

—Johann Wolfgang von Goethe (1749-1832), German playwright, novelist, and scientist

# ACKNOWLEDGEMENTS

Several people helped in the development, research, and creation of this special version of our ESL textbook for The Language Company. Wende Weber, the Director of the Language Company - Berkeley, carefully selected the chapters in this special version of *Compelling Conversations* for the Visiting Scholars and Postdoc Affairs program students. Her dedication and vision made this special edition possible on multiple levels.

This conversation book also reflects the philosophy that "everybody is a student, and everybody is a teacher." Collaboration with many English teachers and English students—from across the globe—in several higher education institutions has continually improved this book with each special edition. The enthusiasm of fellow teachers, students, and friends is a blessing.

Naturally, we also owe an exceptional debt to the dedicated Santa Monica Community College students and the University of Southern California graduate students at the American Language Institute. We have often shared questions, proverbs, and laughs. Our lively conversations, in and out of the classroom, have exceeded expectations. We have often created small classroom communities where we could take chances, develop our skills, and share our personal interests. The adoption of *Compelling Conversations* by the Language Company—in special editions for different skill levels—continues this creative collaboration with English language learners across disciplines and nationalities.

We hope this rich collection of questions, proverbs, and quotations will spark many Compelling Conversations. Let's keep talking, sharing, and learning together!

Eric Roth and Toni Aberson
Co-authors, *Compelling Conversations*

## SPECIAL THANKS

Laurie Selik
Wende Weber
Jim Valentine
Zigmund Vays
Idalia Rodriguez
Adam Rado
Regina Pablo
Sharon Myers
Nina Ito
Alla Kogan
Oleg Khalkevich
Paula Johnson
Ben Hammer
Marina Goldshteyn
Ronit Frazam
Rosa Dreizin
Marc Yablonka
Mai-Anh Nguyen
Leah Montano

**"Gratitude is the memory of the heart."**
—French proverb

# INTRODUCTION

Why do you want to learn English? Are you planning on joining a new university, or making new international friends? Are you hoping to present your research at a professional conference? Are you looking to make more money with international business or travel? Do you want a better job, reach a high TOEFL score, or even become a professor in an English-speaking country?

In all of these situations, speaking clear English and creating smart conversations can open many doors for you in the United States and around the world. English, for worse or for better, is the language of international success and across academic disciplines.

We learn in many ways. We often learn about our world and our selves by simply talking and listening to each other. We also learn by doing and practicing. Sometimes we have short talks; sometime we have long conversations. Sometimes we speak mother tongue; sometimes we speak English.

Together, we will talk about many things in English and discuss many topics in this class in English. We will ask questions in English. We will answer questions in English too. We will use simple and more difficult words in English. We learn traditional sayings and modern expressions. We will learn and use new English vocabulary words in our conversation class. Step by step, we will know more English words and how to ask more questions so we can build better conversations in English.

Learning to speak fluent English requires us to speak English in every class. So we will talk about our present lives and reflect on our past experiences in interviews and small group discussions. We will also share our hopes and plans for the future. By telling our personal stories and sharing our ideas, we will also create compelling conversations together in English.

Shall we begin?

Eric Roth and Toni Aberson
Co-authors, Compelling Conversations

## VITAL ENGLISH LANGUAGE SKILLS

This conversation textbook will gently push you to develop many vital skills:

• Speak English
• Listen to English
• Respond to both questions and comments
• Ask questions
• Learn and use new vocabulary words
• Paraphrase proverbs
• Discuss quotations
• Express opinions
• Support statements
• Begin conversations with native English speakers

**"Colors fade, temples crumble, empires fall, but wise words endure."**
—Edward Thorndike (1874-1949), American psychologist

# TABLE OF CONTENTS

**CHAPTERS**

**APPENDIX**

# CHAPTER 1
# BEING YOURSELF

## SHARING PERSPECTIVES

From consulting charts and reading palms to taking personality tests and reading self-help books, people love to describe themselves.

1. Are you shy or outgoing? When are you most outgoing?

2. Are you daring or cautious? In what ways?

3. Are you usually patient or impatient? Can you give an example?

4. Are you generous or selfish? Are you too selfish or overly generous?

5. In what ways are you rigid? In what ways are you flexible?

6. In what ways are you traditional? In what ways are you modern?

7. If pessimistic is 1 and optimistic is 10, what would your number be on the scale? Why did you decide on that number?

8. On a scale of 1-10, how assertive are you?

## EXPANDING VOCABULARY

| | | | | |
|---|---|---|---|---|
| accurate | character | flexible | generous | nurture |
| patient | optimist | pessimist | rigid | talkative |

**accurate** *adjective*: correct, getting the facts right.

• Scientists, engineers, and doctors must be accurate.

**character** *noun*: one's personality and values; moral sense; a figure in fiction or theater.

• Kelly showed her character at work.

• Oliver Twist is one of my favorite characters in English literature.

**flexible** *adjective*: loose, bending; willing to change.

• Pham is flexible and can work either Friday or Saturday.

**generous**: *adjective*: giving, sharing with others.

• A good sister is generous with her time and helps her family.

**nurture** *verb*: to take care of another; to care for or help someone in need.

• Parents nurture their children and guide them in their lives.

**patient** *adjective*: able to wait calmly, not in a hurry;
**patient** *noun*: a person receiving medical treatment.

• A patient man can calmly wait for a late bus.

• The doctor prescribed medicine for her patient.

**optimist** *noun*: someone who see the positive side and believes things will improve

• She saw the glass as "half-full," which made her an optimist.

**pessimist** *noun*: one who has a negative view, and believes the future will be worse.

• He saw the glass as "half-empty," which made him a pessimist.

**rigid** *adjective*: unwilling to change; inflexible.

• Thomas is so rigid that he will not even listen to other people.

**talkative** *adjective*: verbal; engages in constant or non-stop conversation.

• Tracy becomes talkative when he relaxes with his friends.

### PARAPHRASING PROVERBS

A. Read the following proverbs, and discuss them with your partners. What do they mean? Circle your favorites. Explain your choices.

• Character is destiny.—Greek

• The leopard can not change its spots.—Vietnamese

• Trust yourself.—American

• The more noble, the more humble.—Chinese

• A light heart lives long.—English

• See yourself as others see you.

• A pretty being is better than being pretty.—English

B. Can you add two more?

• .........................................................................................................................

• .........................................................................................................................

1. Do you think our personalities are set when we are born?

2. Can we change our personalities? How?

3. How has your personality changed in the last ten years?

4. Which three words would you use to describe your best friend's personality?

5. How are your personalities similar? How are your personalities different?

6. Why do you think opposites are sometimes attracted to each other?

7. Some cultures define personality in terms of the elements. Would you say you are primarily air, water, fire, or earth? Explain your choice.

8. Which three qualities do you think of as yin (feminine)?

9. Which three qualities do you think of as yang (masculine)?

10. Can you name one yin quality and one yang quality which describe you?

11. How might being raised in poverty influence someone's personality?

12. Would being born in extreme wealth change your personality? How?

13. If you had been born in another country, do you think your personality would be different? How?

14. Can you think of somebody with a good personality and bad character?

15. What is the difference between one's personality and one's character?

16. Are you primarily an extrovert or an introvert? Why do you say that?

17. Do you think nature (biology) or nurture (our circumstances) are more important in shaping our personalities? Why do you say that?

18. What are your best qualities?

## DISCUSSING QUOTATIONS

Take turns reading these quotations out loud, and discuss them with your partners. Do you agree with the quotation? Disagree? Why? Mark your answer. Explain your response.

1. "Know thyself."
   —Socrates (470-399 B.C.E.), Greek philosopher
   ☐ Agree ☐ Disagree Why? ............................................................

2. "The man of character bears the accidents of life with dignity and grace, making the best of circumstances."
   —Aristotle (384–322 B.C.E.), Greek philosopher/ethicist
   ☐ Agree ☐ Disagree Why? ............................................................

## GOALS

Places I want to speak English:

1. ............................................................

2. ............................................................

3. ............................................................

3. "This above all: To thine own self be true, And it must follow, as the night the day, Thou canst not then be false to any man."
—William Shakespeare (1564-1616), English playwright
☐ Agree ☐ Disagree Why? ...........................................................

4. "Character is much easier kept than recovered."
—Thomas Paine (1737–1809), American writer
☐ Agree ☐ Disagree Why? ...........................................................

5. "It is absurd to divide people into good and bad. People are either charming or tedious." —Oscar Wilde (1856–1900), Irish author/playwright
☐ Agree ☐ Disagree Why? ...........................................................

6. "Some people with great virtues are disagreeable, while others with great vice are delightful."
—Francois de la Rochefoucauld (1613—1680), French philosopher
☐ Agree ☐ Disagree Why? ...........................................................

7. "Man's main task in life is to give birth to himself, to become what he potentially is. The most important product of his effort is his own personality."
—Erich Fromm (1900–1980), German-American psychologist
☐ Agree ☐ Disagree Why? ...........................................................

8. "Generous people are rarely mentally ill people."
—Karl Menninger (1893–1990), American psychiatrist
☐ Agree ☐ Disagree Why? ...........................................................

9. "The easiest kind of relationship for me is with ten thousand people. The hardest is with one."
—Joan Baez (1941 - ), American singer
☐ Agree ☐ Disagree Why? ...........................................................

10. "Dwell in possibility."
—Emily Dickinson (1830-1886), American poet
☐ Agree ☐ Disagree Why? ...........................................................

## ★ ON YOUR OWN

What do you like about yourself? Write a postcard to a friend describing your strongest traits:

...........................................................

...........................................................

...........................................................

...........................................................

...........................................................

...........................................................

# CHAPTER 2
# STUDYING ENGLISH

## SHARING EXPERIENCES

English has emerged as the global tongue in the early 21st century. Yet, English remains a crazy, confusing, and misspelled language. Interview a classmate and share your joys and frustrations in learning this important language.

1. Which English words have been adopted into your native language?

2. Where is English most commonly used in your native country? Why?

3. Do advertisements sometimes use English words? Why?

4. When did you first study English? Were you excited, bored, or indifferent?

5. How long have you studied English? What inspired you to study it? Where have you studied English?

6. Have you had any negative experiences learning English?

7. Are there English classes for adults in your country? Are they expensive?

8. What was the best English class you ever had? Why?

9. What method of learning seems to work best for you? Why?

10. Have you found an excellent tool for learning English? What?

## EXPANDING VOCABULARY

Please circle the words that you know, and find meanings of the other words.

| | | | | |
|---|---|---|---|---|
| adopt | inspire | bilingual | audiobook | monolingual |
| eavesdrop | subtitle | examiner | exclusive | offer |

**adopt** *verb*: to accept; to take raise a child not born to your family as your own.

- English has adopted thousands of words–like taco, sushi, czar–from other languages.

**inspire** *verb*: to encourage; motivate other people.

- Keiko wanted to do more than teach—she wanted to inspire her students to achieve great things in their lives.

**"English saved my life."**
—Joseph Conrad(1857-1924), English novelist born in Poland

6

**bilingual** *adjective*: speaking more than one language fluently.

• Being bilingual made it easier for Carlos to find a job during the recession.

**audio book** *noun*: a recorded version of a story or book to be listened to instead of read.

• I enjoy listening to audio books during my long commute to work each day.

**monolingual** *noun*: speaking one language.

• Being monolingual is a disadvantage in our increasingly globalized world.

**eavesdrop** *verb*: to overhear conversation; to listen in secret.

• Sometimes my little brother tries to eavesdrop on my conversations, but I never let him hear.

**subtitle** *noun*: printed translation of a foreign movie at the bottom of the screen; the secondary title of a book.

• The English subtitles helped me understand the Chinese movie because I could read the subtitles.

**examiner** *noun*: someone who assesses or tests people or things.

• They called the medical examiner to determine the cause of death.

**offer** *verb*: to propose, as for an exchange, loan, or gift; to suggest as an idea; *noun*: what is proposed for exchange; a bid.

• I offered Chantou my apartment while I was out of town.

**reform** *verb*: to improve, to transform; *noun*: an improvement or reorganization.

• We need to reform the school system to keep up with technology.

• Some popular political reforms create both positive and negative changes.

### THE CONVERSATION CONTINUES

1. Have you ever called a 1-800-number just to practice your English? What happened?

2. Have you ever listened to an audio book? Which one? Was it enjoyable? Did you learn many new words?

3. Do you ever eavesdrop, or just listen intently, to conversations around you?

4. Do you listen to the radio? Do you have some favorite shows? Why?

5. Do you watch American movies with subtitles? Why?

6. Do you use the closed-captioning feature on many TV programs? Why?

7. Is it easier to spell in English than in your best language? Why?

8. What are some positive aspects of the English language?

9. What are some characteristics that make learning English difficult?

10. Do you have a driver's license? Did you take the exam in English? Why?

11. Should all government agencies exclusively use English? Why or why not?

12. Are you a U.S. citizen? What questions did the examiner ask you?

13. If you were designing the citizenship test, would you change anything? What?

14. What would you not feel comfortable doing in English now?

15. Where would you like to feel more comfortable speaking English?

16. In your opinion, why has English become more popular in the last 20 years?

17. What tips can you offer friends who want to improve their English?

## DISCUSSING QUOTATIONS

Take turns reading these quotations out loud, and discuss them with your partners. Do you agree with the quotation? Disagree? Why? Mark your answer. Explain your response.

1. "I speak two languages, Body and English."
   —Mae West (1892-1980), actress
   ☐ Agree ☐ Disagree Why? ..............................................................................

2. "Words are, of course, the most powerful drug used by mankind."
   —Rudyard Kipling (1865-1936), British author and Nobel laureate
   ☐ Agree ☐ Disagree Why? ..............................................................................

3. "Every immigrant who comes here should be required within five years to learn English or leave the country."
   —Theodore Roosevelt (1858-1919), 26th U.S. President
   ☐ Agree ☐ Disagree Why? ..............................................................................

4. "Even if you do learn to speak correct English, whom are you going to speak it to?"
   —Clarence Darrow (1857-1938), American lawyer
   ☐ Agree ☐ Disagree Why? ..............................................................................

5. "England and America are two countries divided by a common language."
   —George Bernard Shaw (1856-1950), Irish playwright, Nobel Prize winner
   ☐ Agree ☐ Disagree Why? ..............................................................................

6. "Next to money, English is the leading international language."
   —Evan Esar (1899-1995), American humorist
   ☐ Agree ☐ Disagree Why? ..............................................................................

7. " 'Check enclosed' are the most beautiful words in English."
—Dorothy Parker (1893-1967), American writer
☐ Agree ☐ Disagree Why? ........................................................................

8. "The most beautiful words in the English language are 'not guilty.' "
—Maxim Gorky (1868-1936), Russian novelist
☐ Agree ☐ Disagree Why? ........................................................................

9. "The most terrifying words in the English language are: 'I'm from the government and I'm here to help you.'"
—Ronald Reagan (1911-2004), 40th U.S. President
☐ Agree ☐ Disagree Why? ........................................................................

10. "Slang is a language that rolls up its sleeves, spits on the its hands, and goes to work."
—Carl Sandburg (1878-1967), American poet, Folklorist, and historian
☐ Agree ☐ Disagree Why? ........................................................................

11. " 'I am' is reportedly the shortest sentence in the English language. Could it be that 'I do' is the longest sentence?"
—George Carlin (1937-2008), American comedian
☐ Agree ☐ Disagree Why? ........................................................................

12. "In this country, it doesn't make any difference where you were born. It doesn't make any difference who your parents were. It doesn't make any difference if, like me, you couldn't even speak English until you were in your twenties."
—Arnold Schwarzenegger (1947-), California Governor and American actor
☐ Agree ☐ Disagree Why? ........................................................................

## ⭐ ON YOUR OWN

Using only English words, write a favorite food or dish next to each letter. For example: E: Eggs.

E ................................................................

N ................................................................

G ................................................................

L ................................................................

I ................................................................

S ................................................................

H ................................................................

# FINDING ENGLISH PRONUNCIATION TIPS ON YOUTUBE!

Student Name ..............................................................................................................Class..............................

Teacher ................................................................................................................... Date...........................

Find a quality YouTube videoclip that provides a tip on English pronunciation that you would like to share with your classmates. You might look for advice on how to make a particular sound or search for stress patterns. Watch the video, carefully listen, take notes, and share the pronunciation tip with your classmates.

1. Video title: .................................................................................................................................................

2. Web address:.......................................................................................3. Length...........................

4. Creator:.......................................................................................................................................................

5. Please describe the video. Who is the presenter? What happens? .................................................

.........................................................................................................................................................................

.........................................................................................................................................................................

6. What pronunciation tips did the video provide?.................................................................................

.........................................................................................................................................................................

.........................................................................................................................................................................

7. Which words or sounds did the video focus on?.................................................................................

.........................................................................................................................................................................

.........................................................................................................................................................................

8. How practical did you find the advice? Why? ....................................................................................

.........................................................................................................................................................................

9. What was the strongest part? Why?.......................................................................................................

.........................................................................................................................................................................

.........................................................................................................................................................................

10. What was the weakest part? Why? .......................................................................................................

.........................................................................................................................................................................

.........................................................................................................................................................................

11. Who do think is the target audience for this video? ........................................................................

12. Why did you choose this video? ............................................................................................................

.........................................................................................................................................................................

13. How would you rate this video on a 1-to-5 scale? Why?...................................................................

# CHAPTER 3
# PET PEEVES

## SHARING COMPLAINTS

Sometimes things annoy us, and that's okay. Share your complaints and pet peeves with your group. Discussing, sighing, and sharing can sometimes help us in difficult situations.

1. What annoys you? Do you have any pet peeves?

2. Do you prefer sales pitches in person, by phone, on TV, or online? Why?

3. How can salespeople be annoying? Can you give some examples?

4. Have you ever had serious email problems? How did you respond?

5. What behavior do you often find offensive? Why?

6. What is litter? Have you seen any litterbugs?
   Where does litter bother you most?

7. What do you consider bad cell phone manners or habits?

8. When, or where, do you most often see people stressed?

9. What behavior might be considered irritating in a neighbor? Have you ever had a noisy neighbor? Can you give an example of a difficult neighbor?

10. What behavior might be considered strange for a man, but normal for a woman?

## EXPANDING VOCABULARY

| | | | | |
|---|---|---|---|---|
| annoy | bother | courtesy | impolite | litter |
| obnoxious | offended | pet peeve | polite | profanity |

**annoy** *verb*: to disturb or irritate.

• Loud traffic noises annoy me when I'm trying to sleep at night.

**bother** *verb*: to annoy, to disrupt or disturb; to make one feel bad.

• Don't bother me while I'm talking on the phone.

**courtesy** *noun*: a kind or polite act; politeness.

• It's a common courtesy to hold a door open for others.

**"If you don't have anything nice to say, come sit by me."**
—Alice Roosevelt Longworth (1884-1980), icon and Theodore Roosevelt's daughter

**impolite** *adjective*: poor behavior, rude

•It's impolite to spit on the floor.

**litter** *noun*: trash that can be seen on the street; garbage on the ground;
**litter** *verb*: to throw trash on the ground;
**litter** *noun*: a number of dogs or cats born at the same time to the same mother.

• Litter has become a major problem in some large cities with trash all over the streets.

• It's illegal to litter the beach by throwing trash on the sand.

• My dog gave birth to a litter of six puppies.

**obnoxious** *adjective*: extremely annoying; bothersome.

• It's obnoxious to throw leftover food on the street and act like a litterbug.

**offended** *adjective*: feeling upset or insulted.

• I feel offended when you use ugly, vulgar, and rude words to insult me.

**pet peeve** *noun*: something which annoys or irritates a person.

• My biggest pet peeve is my neighbor's loud TV which keeps me awake.

**polite** *adjective*: good manners; respectful.

• Being polite just means thinking about someone else and their feelings.

**profanity** *noun*: a filthy word, offensive language.

• A parent should punish a child who uses profanity in public to insult neighbors.

### PARAPHRASING PROVERBS

A. Read the following proverbs. What do they mean? Circle your favorites. Explain your choices.

• Recite "patience" three times and it will spare you a murder.—Korean

• Hatred is as blind as love."—Irish proverb

• This is done and I'm to blame. Therefore, know that I'm in shame.—Persian

• Control yourself: remember anger is only one letter short of danger. —American high school poster

• Love makes a good eye squint.—English

• The reputation of a thousand years may be determined by the conduct of one hour.—Japanese

• If you empty a cup of wine in one gulp, you are a drunkard.

• So much to do, so little done.

Prepare a one-minute presentation on your biggest pet peeve that you may later give to the class.

B. Can you add two more?

- ............................................................................................................

- ............................................................................................................

**THE CONVERSATION CONTINUES...**

1. What table manners or eating styles make you frown or annoy you?

2. When, if ever, does snoring, sneezing, or coughing bother you?

3. Where do you find adults generally act their worst? Why?

4. How does a polite child act? How does a rude child behave?

5. Where do people learn good manners? What are good manners?

6. What do you dislike about living here?

7. Can you describe a polite boss? A very difficult boss?

8. How have co-workers or classmates annoyed you? What did they do? How did you handle the situation?

9. How have you handled working with rude customers? Are you able to keep your cool?

10. Does foul language, or profanity, upset you? When?

11. What obnoxious behavior have you had a strong negative reaction to?

12. Have you ever walked out of a movie? Were you offended? Why?

13. Are there personality traits that you find extremely disagreeable?

14. How can someone really make you "blow your lid" or explode? What brings out the worst in you? A family relative? A good friend?

15. What once annoyed you that you have, over time, come to tolerate?

16. Have you seen any changes in what are considered good manners? What?

17. What is your advice for dealing with difficult, moody, or "toxic" people?

18. What are some social evils? Why?

19. Can you compare a pet peeve and a social evil?

20. How can people bring out your best side?

## DISCUSSING QUOTATIONS

Take turns reading these quotations aloud, and discuss them with your cohorts. Do you agree with the quotation? Disagree? Mark your answer. Explain your response.

1. "The test of good manners is to be patient with bad ones."
   —Solomon ibn Gabriol (1021–1051), Hebrew poet/philosopher
   ☐ Agree ☐ Disagree Why? ......................................................

2. "Good manners are made up of petty sacrifices."
   —Ralph Waldo Emerson (1803–1882), American essayist
   ☐ Agree ☐ Disagree Why? ......................................................

3. "Be polite; write diplomatically; even in a declaration of war one observes the rules of politeness."
   —Otto von Bismarck (1815–1898), German aristocrat/statesman
   ☐ Agree ☐ Disagree Why? ......................................................

4. "Never treat a guest like a member of the family—treat him with courtesy."
   —Evan Esar (1899–1935), American humorist
   ☐ Agree ☐ Disagree Why? ......................................................

5. "Isn't it monstrous the way people go about saying things behind other people's backs that are absolutely and entirely true?"
   —Oscar Wilde (1854–1900), Irish author/playwright
   ☐ Agree ☐ Disagree Why? ......................................................

6. "When you're down and out, something always turns up—usually the noses of your friends."
   —Orson Welles (1915–1985), American actor/director
   ☐ Agree ☐ Disagree Why? ......................................................

7. "Those who do not complain are never pitied."
   —Jane Austen (1775-1819), English novelist
   ☐ Agree ☐ Disagree Why? ......................................................

8. "There are bad manners everywhere, but an aristocracy is bad manners organized."
   —Henry James (1843-1916), American writer
   ☐ Agree ☐ Disagree Why? ......................................................

9. "Kindness is the language which the deaf can hear and the blind can see."
   —Mark Twain (1835-1910), American writer
   ☐ Agree ☐ Disagree Why? ......................................................

10. "I have the simplest taste. I am always satisfied with the best."
    —Oscar Wilde (1854-1900), Irish writer
    ☐ Agree ☐ Disagree Why? ......................................................

## ⭐ ON YOUR OWN

Write three consumer complaints with a preposition.

1. ......................................................
......................................................
......................................................

2. ......................................................
......................................................
......................................................

3. ......................................................
......................................................
......................................................

Write three responses to consumer complaints with prepositions.

1. ......................................................
......................................................
......................................................

2. ......................................................
......................................................
......................................................

3. ......................................................
......................................................
......................................................

# CUSTOMER COMPLAINTS AND PRACTICING PREPOSITIONS

We often need to use proper English to solve problems at work. Work with your conversation partner and find the right preposition to fill in the missing blank. Take turns reading sentences and determine which sentences are replies to complaints. The prepositions are grouped together for clarity. After filling in each group determine whether the speaker is making a complaint or responding to a complaint.

## To

- I'm writing ........... complain about your customer service helpline.
- I'm calling ........... make a complaint.
- I wish ........... make an inquiry about something on my monthly bill.
- I've been trying ........... get through to you for two weeks.
- The order was delivered ........... the wrong branch.
- I'm sorry that I didn't get back ........... you sooner.
- The delay wasn't our fault. It was due ........... the bad weather.

## On

- The delivery arrived ........... the wrong day.
- If you can't deliver ........... time, we'll have to contact other suppliers.
- I would like to apologize ........... behalf of Nippon Ham for any inconvenience.

## For

- Please accept our apologies ........... the inconvenience.
- We would like to offer you a discount on your next order to make up ........... our mistake.
- Thank you ........... bringing this matter to my attention.
- I'm sorry ........... sending the documents to the wrong address.
- Who signed ........... the delivery?

## Of

- Please find a list ........... the missing items.
- There were a number ........... mistakes on the invoice.
- Several ........... our delivery vehicles are out of service.
- We were closed for a number ........... days due to the floods.

## About

- I'm sorry. I'm calling to complain ........... your payment system.
- I'm calling ........... my order. It isn't here yet.
- I'd like to learn ........... your refund policy.

## Under

- The product is no longer ........... warranty.
- We found your order ........... someone else's name.
- Would you please look ........... the counter to see if there are more?
- I'd like to see the shirt ........... the blue one.

## With

- I had some problems ........... the instruction booklet.
- ........... reference to your reminder of December 1, it seems to us that an error has been made.
- We are not satisfied ........... the quality of the products.
- I have checked ........... the staff involved, and they claim they were not responsible.

## In

- ........... fact, we had already paid the full bill the previous week.
- We will do our best to ensure that such mistakes do not occur again ........... the future.
- Are you sure it was included ........... the shipment?

## Into

- We will look ........... it right away and get back to you as soon as we can.
- I would be grateful if you could look ........... the matter.

## At

- I believe your sales department is ........... fault.
- Would you please look _____ the bill I received?
- Our records show the package was received ___ your address.

## By

- We strongly believe that the mistake was made ........... your company.
- We will correct the mistake ........... noon today.
- The part will be replaced ........... the manufacturer.

### EXERCISE

Write three consumer complaints with a preposition.

1..................................................................................................................................................
2..................................................................................................................................................
3..................................................................................................................................................

Write three responses to consumer complaints with prepositions.

1..................................................................................................................................................
2..................................................................................................................................................
3..................................................................................................................................................

# CHAPTER 4
# HOLIDAYS AND CELEBRATIONS

## SHARING MEMORIES

Holidays bring people together. Talk with your group about the holidays of your lives.

1. When you were a child, what was your favorite holiday or festival? Why? What did you enjoy?

2. What inspired this holiday? What usually happens on this holiday?

3. What are some holy days in your religious tradition?

4. In your native land, is there a special day to honor mothers? Fathers? Children?

5. Can you think of a fantasy figure, such as Santa Claus, connected to holiday celebrations? What is the fantasy figure like? What does this fantasy figure do?

6. What are the official legal holidays in your native country?

7. What are the 10 official, legal holidays in the United States?

## EXPANDING VOCABULARY

Please circle the words that you know. Use them to write three questions.

| celebrate | festival | fireworks | carol | accompany |
| celebration | costumes | veteran | ritual | procession |

**celebrate** *verb*: to show happiness for an occasion; to mark a special event such as a wedding or birth.

• You are invited to a party to celebrate the birth of my first child.

**festival** *noun*: a large-scale celebration.

• Every summer they have a week-long jazz festival at the beach.

**fireworks** *noun*: explosives meant for display and entertainment; pyrotechnic explosions set off to celebrate something; excitement between people.

• We always have fireworks on Independence Day.

**carol** *noun*: a religious song or hymn.

19

..........................................................

..........................................................

..........................................................

..........................................................

..........................................................

..........................................................

..........................................................

• Every Christmas she led a group through the village singing carols.

**accompany** *verb*: to go with someone; to play music for another person's performance.

• Will you accompany me to the charity event?

**celebration** *noun*: a happy event, like a festival, to mark something festive.

• We were so happy to finish school, the celebration went on until dawn.

**costumes** *noun*: special items of clothing worn to change a person's appearance; a disguise; clothing worn for a particular event or holiday.

• When we perform our traditional dances, we wear the same costumes our ancestors wore.

**veteran** *noun*: a soldier or other person who served in the nation's armed forces; an experienced person.

• My father was a veteran of the Vietnam War.

**ritual** *noun*: a particular action or religious ceremony or part of a ceremonial event; a repeated action or habit.

• Drinking two cups of coffee is part of my morning ritual.

**procession** *noun*: a group of people moving in a line, usually in a commemoration or religious celebration;

• There were many mourners in the funeral procession.

### PARAPHRASING PROVERBS

A. We have many expressions about holidays. Read the following expressions, and discuss them with your partners. What do they mean? Circle your favorites. Explain your choices.

• The more the merrier.
• When the boss is away, work becomes a holiday. —Portuguese
• Time spent laughing is time spent with the gods. —Japanese
• Enjoy yourself. It's later than you think. —Chinese
• Shared joys are doubled; shared sorrows are halved.

B. Can you add two more proverbs about food?

• ....................................................................................................................

• ....................................................................................................................

### THE CONVERSATION CONTINUES

1. What are some traditional gifts for Valentine's Day? How do you celebrate it?

2. Do you know what happens in the comic movie *Groundhog Day*?

3. Which holidays include special songs, dances, or costumes?

4. Do you have a favorite song or dance linked to a holiday? Which? Do you own any collection of holiday songs?

5. Which holidays often include fireworks? Parades? Caroling?

6. What are three special holiday activities for children?

7. On what holidays, do people traditionally put on costumes? Did you celebrate a holiday similar to Halloween in your native country?

8. What are some holidays that occur in the Spring?

9. Do you have a favorite Spring holiday? What is it? How is it celebrated?

10. In your native land, is there a winter holiday which uses lots of lights near the winter solstice? What is the holiday? How is it celebrated?

11. Now that you are in the U.S., do you still celebrate the same holidays?

12. Can you think of some movies centered around a holiday? Do you have a favorite movie to watch during the holidays? Why?

13. What is your favorite holiday? How do you celebrate it?

14. Have you seen any new holidays created, or dropped, in your lifetime? Which ones?

15. Do you feel more homesick near holiday time? What do you miss?

16. Why do you think so many people find the holiday season stressful?

17. What are your best tips to make holidays a positive experience?

18. Would you like to add, or create, a new holiday? What? Why? How would you like to celebrate this new holiday?

## DISCUSSING QUOTATIONS

Take turns reading these quotations out loud, and discuss them with your partners. Do you agree with the quotation? Disagree? Why? Mark your answer. Explain your response.

1. "A feast is made for laughter."
   —Ecclesiastes 10:19.
   ☐ Agree ☐ Disagree Why? ...........................................................

2. "You can't have Thanksgiving without turkey. That's like Fourth of July without apple pie, or Friday without two pizzas."
   —Joey (Matt LeBlanc) on Friends, a TV situation comedy (sitcom) series
   ☐ Agree ☐ Disagree Why? ...........................................................

3. "Happy, happy Christmas, that win us back to the delusions of our childhood days, recall to the old man the pleasures of his youth, and transport the traveler back to his own fireside and quiet home."
—Charles Dickens (1812-1870) English novelist
☐ Agree ☐ Disagree Why? ........................................................

4. "I was an atheist for a while, but I gave it up. No holidays!"
—Henry Youngman (1906-1998) American comedian
☐ Agree ☐ Disagree Why? ........................................................

5. "In the old days, it was not called the Holiday Season; the Christians called it 'Christmas' and went to church; the Jews called it 'Hanukkah' and went to synagogue; the atheists went to parties and drank."
—Dave Barry (1947-) American comedian
☐ Agree ☐ Disagree Why? ........................................................

6. "Christmas is the season when gifts are gladly given, happily received, and cheerfully refunded."
—Evan Esar (1899-1995), American humorist
☐ Agree ☐ Disagree Why? ........................................................

7. "April 1: This is the day upon which we are reminded of what we are on the other three hundred and sixty-four."
—Mark Twain (1835-1910) humorist
☐ Agree ☐ Disagree Why? ........................................................

8. "Live your life while you have it. Life is a splendid gift-there's nothing small about it."
—Florence Nightingale (1820-1910), Founder of the Red Cross
☐ Agree ☐ Disagree Why? ........................................................

9. "Yes, Virginia, there is a Santa Claus. He exists as certainly as love and generosity and devotion exist."
—Francis B. Church (1839-1906), publisher and editor
☐ Agree ☐ Disagree Why?

10. "Today is Valentine's Day, or, as men like to call it, Extortion Day!"
—Jay Leno (1950-), late night American television comedian
☐ Agree ☐ Disagree Why?

11. "To many people holidays are not voyages of discovery, but a ritual of reassurance."
—Phillip Andrew Adams (1939-), Australian broadcaster
☐ Agree ☐ Disagree Why? ........................................................

## ⭐ ON YOUR OWN

On a plain sheet of paper, create a calendar for the month of your birth, showing your birthday and other holidays.

Then, on separate sheets of paper, create a 12-month calendar showing the days you celebrate and official American holidays.

# EXPLORING MORE HOLIDAYS!

Student Name ........................................................................................................ Date...........................

Class............................................................................................. Teacher............................

Please search for an article on the Internet (in English) about a favorite holiday or celebration. Please choose a holiday that you do not currently celebrate, but that you would like to know more about. Find an article, read it, print it out, and be prepared to discuss it with classmates.

Title .................................................................................................................................

Author: ...................................................................................Length...........................

Publication: .............................................................................Publication date........................

What is the name of the holiday or celebration you have chosen? .................................................

What are two or three important facts about the holiday or celebration?........................................

.................................................................................................................................

.................................................................................................................................

Who is quoted in this article? How are they identified? ..........................................................

.................................................................................................................................

What did you learn about a new holiday from this article?........................................................

.................................................................................................................................

What was the most interesting part for you? Why?................................................................

.................................................................................................................................

Write down 5 new vocabulary words, idioms, or expressions.

1. ............................................................................................................................

2. ............................................................................................................................

3. ............................................................................................................................

4. ............................................................................................................................

5. ............................................................................................................................

How would you rate this video on a scale of 1-5? Why? ..........................................................

.................................................................................................................................

Why did you choose this article?.....................................................................................

.................................................................................................................................

.................................................................................................................................

# CHAPTER 5

# EATING OUT

## SHARING EXPERIENCES

Do you know any good restaurants? Share with your class what you have learned about eating out.

1. Where are some places to eat out in your neighborhood?

2. What kinds of ethnic food do you enjoy? Do you have a favorite dish?

3. Do you prefer eating out with a single person or with a group?

4. Do you drink alcohol when you eat out? Do you have a favorite drink?

5. Do you regularly eat out with friends? How often do eat out?

6. Why do you think fast food restaurants are so popular?

## EXPANDING VOCABULARY

Are any of these words new to you? Circle them. Does your partner know their meaning? Can you figure out their meaning?

| | | | | |
|---|---|---|---|---|
| menu | reservation | busboy | waiters | cuisine |
| host | valet | split plate | manners. | |

**menu** *noun*: A list of all the food available to order in a restaurant.

• There are so many choices on the menu it's hard to decide what to order.

**reservation** *noun*: an arrangement you make for a table or space to be held for you.

• My wife had to make reservations six months ago to get a table at this bistro.

**busboy** *noun*: a person at a restaurant who cleans up the table, brings water, and clears dishes.

• Bruno began as a busboy, but soon worked his way up to being a waiter at a fine restaurant.

**waiters** *noun*: people that wait on the customer in a restaurant.

• The steak was undercooked so I asked the waiter to take it back.

**"Gluttony is not a secret vice."**
—Orson Welles (1915-1985), great director/actor

**cuisine** *noun*: a category of food; a style of cooking.

• My husband likes Italian food, but my favorite cuisine is Middle Eastern.

**host** *noun*: a person who invites people for food, drink or entertainment, a person who show you to your table at a restaurant.

• The host said we would have to wait twenty minutes for a table.

**valet** *noun*: a person parks your car at a restaurant.

• I gave my ticket to the valet so he could bring my car to me.

**split plate** *noun*: sharing a meal between two people.

• Jackie's favorite restaurant charges extra for a split plate.

**manners** *noun*: etiquette; conventions of politeness, courtesy.

• You showed fine manners at the dinner table by waiting until everyone was served before you began eating.

### THE CONVERSATION CONTINUES

1. Have you ever ordered off the menu? Why?

2. What can go wrong in a restaurant? Have you ever been disappointed? Have you ever sent food back? Have you ever gotten sick from restaurant food?

3. Do you usually tip waiters? How much?

4. Have you ever worked as a host, chef, waiter, or manager in a restaurant?

5. What was the best part of working in the restaurant? The worst?

6. Do you have a favorite restaurant which serves food from your native country?

7. What language do you use when you order food at that restaurant? Why?

8. How are manners different when dining out in your native country?

9. Did you go out to eat more in your native country than here or vice versa?

10. What are some advantages of home cooking? Do you find cooking a chore or a pleasure?

11. What are some advantages of eating out?

12. How do you judge, evaluate, or rate restaurants?

13. Can you suggest some local restaurants for a romantic dinner?

14. Can you recall any memorable restaurant scenes in famous movies?

15. What are some of your favorite restaurant memories?

Take turns reading these quotations out loud, and discuss them with your partners. Do you agree with the quotation? Disagree? Why? Mark your answer. Explain your response.

1. "There's no sauce in the world like hunger."
   —Miquel De Cervantes (1547-1616) Spanish writer
   ☐ Agree ☐ Disagree Why? ........................................................

2. "Get to know the chef and you will start to enjoy dining out even more."
   —John Walters, (1938-2001), British radio producer and musician
   ☐ Agree ☐ Disagree Why? ........................................................

3. "I judge a restaurant by the bread and the coffee."
   —Burt Lancaster (1915-1994), American actor
   ☐ Agree ☐ Disagree Why? ........................................................

4. "I do adore food. If I have any vice it's eating. If I was told I could only eat one food for the rest of my life, I could put up with sausage and mash forever."
   —Colin Baker (1943-), British actor
   ☐ Agree ☐ Disagree Why? ........................................................

5. "He may live without books-what is knowledge but grieving? He may live without hope-what is hope but deceiving? He may live without love-what is passion but pining? But where is the man who can live without dining?"
   —Edward Bulwer-Lytton (1831-1891), poet
   ☐ Agree ☐ Disagree Why? ........................................................

6. "I have never developed indigestion from eating my words."
   —Winston Churchill (1874-1965), British Prime Minister
   ☐ Agree ☐ Disagree Why? ........................................................

7. "I have dined with kings, I've been offered wings. And I've never been too impressed."
   —Bob Dylan (1941-), American folksinger
   ☐ Agree ☐ Disagree Why? ........................................................

8. "Gastronomical perfection can be reached in these combinations: one person dining alone, usually upon a couch or a hill side; two people, of no matter what sex or age, dining in a good restaurant; six people dining in a good home."
   —M.F.K. Fisher (1908-1992), culinary writer
   ☐ Agree ☐ Disagree Why? ........................................................

9. "I've known what it is to be hungry, but I always went right to a restaurant."—Ring Lardner (1885-1933) American writer

☐ Agree ☐ Disagree Why? .........................................................

10. "The best fame is a writer's fame. It's enough to get a table at a good restaurant, but not enough to get you interrupted when you eat."
—Fran Lebowitz (1950-), writer

☐ Agree ☐ Disagree Why? .........................................................

11. "The other night I ate at a real nice family restaurant. Every table had an argument going."
—George Carlin (1937-2008) American comedian

☐ Agree ☐ Disagree Why? .........................................................

12. "I learned more from the one restaurant that didn't work than from all the others that were successes."—Wolfgang Puck (1949-), chef

☐ Agree ☐ Disagree Why? .........................................................

13. "Dining is and always was a great artistic opportunity."
—Frank Lloyd Wright (1867-1959), American architect

☐ Agree ☐ Disagree Why? .........................................................

14. "One cannot think well, love well, sleep well, if one has not dined well."
—Virginia Woolf, (1882-1941), English novelist

☐ Agree ☐ Disagree Why? .........................................................

## ⭐ ON YOUR OWN

With your partners, role play a good waiter and a difficult customer. Then, role play a pleasant customer and a difficult waiter.

# A NIGHT OUT AT A FANCY RESTAURANT

### ROLE PLAY PREPARATION: ASKING QUESTIONS

Eating out can be fun and satisfying, especially if ordering in English.

What are three typical questions to ask a waiter at a nice restaurant?

1.........................................................................................................................................................

2.........................................................................................................................................................

3.........................................................................................................................................................

What are three questions you might ask a friend at dinner?

1.........................................................................................................................................................

2.........................................................................................................................................................

3.........................................................................................................................................................

### ROLE PLAY: ACCIDENTS HAPPEN!

Everybody wants to have a good time when they go out, but sometimes bad things happen to good people—even in nice restaurants!

Let's imagine this situation: Two friends are going to dinner, and they want to talk. At the restaurant, a new waiter has just started. He's very nervous. It's a busy night at a fashionable restaurant on Saturday night. Everybody wants to have a good time, but accidents do happen.

What will happen? ........................................................................................................................................

Who are the friends? .....................................................................................................................................

What do they want to talk about? ..................................................................................................................

What's the restaurant's name?........................................................................................................................

Where is the restaurant? ...............................................................................................................................

Who is the waiter? ........................................................................................................................................

Why is the restaurant so busy?......................................................................................................................

What accidents will happen?.........................................................................................................................

What will happen next?..................................................................................................................................

Can you create a fun skit? Answer the questions and act in your own play. Have fun.

CHAPTER NOTES

# CHAPTER 6

# WHAT DO YOU THINK?

## BRIDGING DIFFERENCES

Harmony is often important, but sometimes we still find ourselves disagreeing with loved ones, close friends, and co-workers. Therefore, we have to find ways to resolve the conflict in a respectful way. Sometimes we just listen and postpone an awkward discussion. Sometimes we try to find agreement and focus on where we agree. And sometimes we need to identify and express our disagreement so we can solve problems together.

The following phrases let you state your position clearly while keeping the conversation friendly. Read all phrases aloud.

| Expressing agreement | Expressing disagreement |
| --- | --- |
| That's right. | Sorry, I disagree. |
| Absolutely. | I partially agree. |
| That's true. | That doesn't seem completely true. |
| I believe that. | Sorry, I don't share that belief. |
| That's a good idea. | While that sounds good, it may not work. |
| This explains A, B, and C. | What about X, Y, or Z? |
| That's right on point. | That seems a bit off point. |
| I concur. | Sorry, I can't completely agree. |
| I agree. | I don't agree. |
| That's valid. | That's invalid. |
| I accept that. | I reject that. |
| I support that. | I don't support that idea. |
| That's a good idea! | Here's a better idea! |
| I definitely agree. | I'm not sure I agree. |
| You should agree with me. | We agree on some points. |
| That sounds logical. | Is that really logical? |
| It's simple. | Or is it complicated? |

"In the middle of a difficulty lies opportunity."
—Albert Einstein (1879 -1955), Time Magazine Man of the 20th Century

accept     acceptance     agreement     disagreement   assume
assumption   concur          consequences  solve          solution

**Accept** *verb*: to say yes, to agree, to concur.

• Thuy accepted the invitation to dinner.

**Acceptance** *noun*: the act of agreeing, the act of receiving something offered.

• Mariam's acceptance of his marriage proposal made everyone smile.

**Agreement** *noun*: the act of agreeing, a contract.

• The agreement was fair so we signed it.

**Disagreement** *noun*: the act of disagreeing, having different ideas and emotions.

• The disagreement seems silly now, but we were very upset at the time.

**Assume** *verb*: to accept without evidence, to believe without question.

• Let's assume that all parents love children, and always want the best for them.

**Assumption** *noun*: the act of taking something for granted, an unquestioned idea.

• The assumption that "newer means better" can sometimes be wrong.

**Concur** *verb*: to agree with, to support.

• Henry concurred with his co-workers that they were lucky to have good jobs.

**Consequences** *noun*: the result or outcome of something.

• Alice's decision to move to the United States had many consequences.

**Solve** *verb*: to find the answer, to work something out.

• Engineers solve problems by examining facts, considering alternatives, and making calculations.

**Solution** *noun*: the act of solving problems, finding answers.

• The simplest solution is sometimes the best solution, but sometimes the simplest solution doesn't really solve the problem.

Do you agree or disagree with the following proverbs? Why? Discuss with your partner.

1. The best things in life are free.
   ☐ Agree ☐ Disagree Why? ........................................................

2. Children should be seen and not heard.
   ☐ Agree ☐ Disagree Why? ........................................................

3. Spare the rod and spoil the child.
   ☐ Agree ☐ Disagree Why? ........................................................

4. Money is the root of all evil.
   ☐ Agree ☐ Disagree Why? ........................................................

5. Honesty is the best policy.
   ☐ Agree ☐ Disagree Why? ........................................................

6. It's better to have loved and lost than never to have loved at all.
   ☐ Agree ☐ Disagree Why? ........................................................

7. Behind every successful man there's a woman.
   ☐ Agree ☐ Disagree Why? ........................................................

8. The end justifies the means.
   ☐ Agree ☐ Disagree Why? ........................................................

9. Winning is everything.
   ☐ Agree ☐ Disagree Why? ........................................................

10. Better to be a live dog than a dead lion.
    ☐ Agree ☐ Disagree Why? ........................................................

11. Persistence pays.
    ☐ Agree ☐ Disagree Why? ........................................................

12. There is no good war and no bad peace.
    ☐ Agree ☐ Disagree Why? ........................................................

13. Your best friend is yourself.
    ☐ Agree ☐ Disagree Why? ........................................................

14. Never judge a movie by its preview.
    ☐ Agree ☐ Disagree Why? ........................................................

15. You can't keep a good man down.
    ☐ Agree ☐ Disagree Why? ........................................................

16. A closed mouth catches no flies.

☐ Agree ☐ Disagree Why? ......................................................

17. The best defense is a good offense.

☐ Agree ☐ Disagree Why? ......................................................

18. Money makes the world go round.

☐ Agree ☐ Disagree Why? ......................................................

## PERSUADING WITH PROVERBS

Choose a proverb from the previous section about which you and your conversation partners disagree. Spend five minutes thinking of situations to support your point of view to persuade your conversation partners.

Then discuss your opinions in a friendly, respectful way. Use some of the phrases at the beginning of this chapter to keep the conversation flowing. Write down the proverb that you will discuss.

## SEEKING CLARIFICATION

Sometimes we need more information to better understand each other, and reach an agreement. Read each of these phrases aloud to your partners.

• Can you clarify that?

• Can you explain your ideas more?

• So?

• What do you mean?

• Can you rephrase that?

• Why do you say that?

• Can you give another example?

• Have you considered?

• What if the situation were a bit different?

• What if?

• How far would you go?

• Are you sure? Why are you so sure?

• What's your source for that bit of information?

• How do you know?

• Can you imagine some alternatives?

• Is there another possibility?

Consider each of the following common statements, attitudes, or proverbs. Which statement of agreement or disagreement best expresses your reaction?

1. Seeing is believing.
   ☐ Agree ☐ Disagree Why? ........................................................

2. Appearances are deceiving.
   ☐ Agree ☐ Disagree Why? ........................................................

3. Beauty promises happiness.
   ☐ Agree ☐ Disagree Why? ........................................................

4. Be good and you will be happy.
   ☐ Agree ☐ Disagree Why? ........................................................

5. No pain, no gain.
   ☐ Agree ☐ Disagree Why? ........................................................

6. No pain, no pain.
   ☐ Agree ☐ Disagree Why? ........................................................

7. The bigger, the better.
   ☐ Agree ☐ Disagree Why? ........................................................

8. Less is more.
   ☐ Agree ☐ Disagree Why? ........................................................

9. Cream rises to the top.
   ☐ Agree ☐ Disagree Why? ........................................................

10. The unexpected always happens.
    ☐ Agree ☐ Disagree Why? ........................................................

11. You get what you pay for.
    ☐ Agree ☐ Disagree Why? ........................................................

12. A penny saved is a penny earned.
    ☐ Agree ☐ Disagree Why? ........................................................

13. Two can live as cheaply as one.
    ☐ Agree ☐ Disagree Why? ........................................................

14. Bad news travels fast.
    ☐ Agree ☐ Disagree Why? ........................................................

15. Liars should have good memories.
    ☐ Agree ☐ Disagree Why? ........................................................

16. Life is not a popularity contest.
☐ Agree ☐ Disagree Why? .....................................................

17. Counting your money is how you keep score.
☐ Agree ☐ Disagree Why? .....................................................

18. You can't take it with you.
☐ Agree ☐ Disagree Why? .....................................................

19. Time heals all wounds.
☐ Agree ☐ Disagree Why? .....................................................

20. Never forget; never forgive.
☐ Agree ☐ Disagree Why? .....................................................

21. Don't throw your pearls before swine.
☐ Agree ☐ Disagree Why? .....................................................

22. A donkey prefers hay to gold.
☐ Agree ☐ Disagree Why? .....................................................

## ASKING QUESTIONS WITH PROVERBS

We've studied proverbs throughout this book. Ask five questions using a proverb. Example: Do you agree that time heals all wounds?

1. .....................................................................................

.....................................................................................

2. .....................................................................................

.....................................................................................

3. .....................................................................................

.....................................................................................

4. .....................................................................................

.....................................................................................

5. .....................................................................................

.....................................................................................

Take turns reading these quotations out loud, and discuss them with your partners. Do you agree with the quotation? Disagree? Why? Mark your answer. Explain your response.

1. "True love is like ghosts, which everybody talks about and few have seen."
   —Francois Duc De La Rochefoucauld (1613-1680), French writer
   ☐ Agree ☐ Disagree Why? .........................................................

2. "Do not anticipate trouble or worry about what may never happen. Keep in the sunlight."
   —Benjamin Franklin (1705-1790), American statesman/scientist
   ☐ Agree ☐ Disagree Why? .........................................................

3. "Nobody minds having what is too good for them."
   —Jane Austen (1775-1821), English novelist
   ☐ Agree ☐ Disagree Why? .........................................................

4. "Nothing is so dangerous as an ignorant friend; a wise enemy is much better."
   —Jean de La Fontaine (1621-1695), French poet
   ☐ Agree ☐ Disagree Why? .........................................................

5. "It is only with the heart that one can see rightly; what is essential is invisible to the eye."
   — Antoine de Saint-Exupery (1900 – 1944), French writer and pilot
   ☐ Agree ☐ Disagree Why? .........................................................

6. "It was the best of times; it was the worst of times."
   —Charles Dickens (1812-1870), English novelist
   ☐ Agree ☐ Disagree Why? .........................................................

7. "If two ride on a horse, one must ride behind."
   —William Shakespeare (1564-1616), great English playwright
   ☐ Agree ☐ Disagree Why?

8. "Experience is the name everyone gives their mistakes."
   —Oscar Wilde (1854-1900), Irish playwright
   ☐ Agree ☐ Disagree Why? .........................................................

9. "Always do the right thing. This will gratify some and astonish the rest."
   —Mark Twain (1835-1910), American writer
   ☐ Agree ☐ Disagree Why? .........................................................

10. "A problem is a chance for you to do your best."
    —Duke Ellington (1890-1974), Jazz composer and band leader
    ☐ Agree ☐ Disagree Why? .........................................................

## ⭐ ON YOUR OWN

Learning to politely discuss and solve problems is a vital workplace skill. We should, for instance, always carefully listen to make sure we understand a problem before we express our opinion.

Write five other guidelines that people can follow to have productive, positive conversations when they disagree about something. Be prepared to explain your answers.

1. ................................................
2. ................................................
3. ................................................
4. ................................................
5. ................................................

# PROBLEM-SOLUTION WORKSHEET

The English proverb "two heads are better than one" is often true. Solving problems can often be difficult. Working with your partner, focus on a problem—at school, at work, or in the local city—and find a reasonable solution together. Please follow this classic problem-solution method widely used in engineering and the sciences to solve problems. Be ready to share your process and conclusions in a short presentation next class.

## DEFINE THE PROBLEM

Background .................................................................................................................................

Problem .....................................................................................................................................

Short-term effects .....................................................................................................................

Long-term effects......................................................................................................................

## FIND THE BEST SOLUTION

Possible solution .......................................................................................................................

• Advantage...............................................................................................................................

• Disadvantage ..........................................................................................................................

Possible solution .......................................................................................................................

• Advantage...............................................................................................................................

• Disadvantage ..........................................................................................................................

Possible solution .......................................................................................................................

• Advantage...............................................................................................................................

• Disadvantage ..........................................................................................................................

Possible solution .......................................................................................................................

• Advantage...............................................................................................................................

• Disadvantage ..........................................................................................................................

Best Solution .............................................................................................................................

Reasons:

1. .............................................................................................................................................

2. .............................................................................................................................................

3. .............................................................................................................................................

# CHAPTER 7

# CHANGE

### SHARING NOTES

All of us have to deal with change. Sometimes it's fun; sometimes it's hard. Share some of your experiences with your class partners.

1. How have clothing fashions changed during your lifetime?

2. How have your looks changed in the last ten years?

3. What type of technology has helped the most people? Why?

4. What political changes have happened in your native country in your lifetime?

5. What is a custom or tradition that you would like to change in your native country? Why?

6. What three political changes would you like to happen in the world?

### EXPANDING VOCABULARY

Circle the words that you already actively use. Review the other words.

| | | | | |
|---|---|---|---|---|
| fashion | makeover | inevitable | adjust | resist |
| resistance | rehabilitation | optimistic | pessimistic | resilient |

**fashion** *noun*: a style of appearance usually involving clothing or hairstyle.
**fashion** *verb*: to design or build.

• She stood out in a crowd because she always wore fashions from the 1940s.

He walked in a slow, deliberate fashion.

**makeover** *noun*: the result of a dramatic alteration in appearance.

• She changed her hairstyle, make-up, and clothes—it was a complete makeover.

**inevitable** *adjective*: something impossible to avoid, predictable.

• It was inevitable that they would meet again because they went to the same small university.

**"Nothing is constant except change."**
—Heraclitus (ca. 513 B.C.E.), Greek philosopher

**adjust** *verb*: to change or modify; to alter to be more exact or fitting.

• When you drive my car, you'll need to adjust the mirror to your height.

**resist** *verb*: to fight back against something; to repress or push back an impulse.

• I couldn't resist having a little chocolate after my meal.

**resistance** *noun*: the act of resisting, pushing back against a force.

• The French Resistance movement fought the German occupation of France.

**rehabilitation** *noun*: repair by training or therapy, restoration of a person after an injury or disease; reform or redemption, the restoration of character or morality.

• Some addicts get better when they attend rehabilitation programs.

**optimistic** *adjective*: taking a hopeful, positive view of the future; looking at the positive.

• He was optimistic about the rain ending so he didn't take an umbrella.

**pessimistic** *adjective*: taking a negative view of the future; looking at the negative.

• Carmen was so pessimistic about passing the test she was shocked to get a good grade.

**resilient** *adjective*: able to recover quickly, spring back.

• The coach was amazed at how resilient his star player was, coming back so quickly after such a serious injury.

## PARAPHRASING PROVERBS, IDIOMS, AND PUNS

A. We have many expressions about change, and some word jokes. Read the following expressions, and discuss them with your partners. What do they mean? Circle your favorites. Explain your choices.

• Don't change horses in midstream.
• A leopard can't change its spots.
• Change is in the air.
• It's time for a change.
• Will this change put some change in my pockets?
• A bird in the hand is worth two in the bush.
• The grass is always greener on the other side of the fence.
• Old habits die hard.
• Change for change's sake.
• You can't make an omelette without breaking eggs.
• Out with the old and in with the new.
• You can't teach an old dog new tricks.
• It's a woman's prerogative to change her mind.

B. Can you add two more proverbs about change?

- ...........................................................................................................

- ...........................................................................................................

## THE CONVERSATION CONTINUES...

1. Can you name anything which is the same as it was 100 years ago? What?

2. What personal changes would you welcome?

3. Are there personal changes that you fear? What?

4. If you could stop time and keep everything the same, would you? Why?

5. What change in your life did you easily adjust to?

6. What change did you resist? Did it work? Was resistance helpful?

7. Have any of your basic ideas changed in the last five years? What?

8. Do you believe that rehabilitation is possible for violent criminals?

9. What changes do you think will happen in the next five years? Why?

10. What changes do you hope for in the next decade? 100 years?

11. Have your ideas about family changed as you have grown older? How?

12. Have your ideas about God changed as you have grown older? How?

13. Have your ideas about happiness changed as you have grown older? How?

14. Are you more optimistic or more pessimistic than you used to be? Why? Can you give an example?

15. Can you share some tips for becoming more resilient amidst change?

## DISCUSSING QUOTATIONS

Take turns reading these quotations out loud, and discuss them with your partners. Do you agree with the quotation? Disagree? Why? Mark your answer. Explain your response.

1. "The universe is change."
   —Marcus Aurelius (121-180), Roman Emperor
   ☐ Agree ☐ Disagree Why? ..........................................................

2. "Never doubt that a small group of thoughtful, committed citizens can change the world. Indeed it is the only thing that ever has."
   —Margaret Mead (1907-1978), anthropologist
   ☐ Agree ☐ Disagree Why? ..........................................................

3. "Change your thoughts and you change the world."
   —Norman Vincent Peale (1898-1993), clergyman
   ☐ Agree ☐ Disagree Why? ..........................................................

4. "There is nothing like returning to a place that remains unchanged to find the ways in which you yourself have altered."
   —Nelson Mandela (1918-), African Leader
   ☐ Agree ☐ Disagree Why? ......................................................

5. "Things do not change; we change."
   —Henry David Thoreau (1817-1862), essayist
   ☐ Agree ☐ Disagree Why? ......................................................

6. "Time may change me, but I can't change time."
   —David Bowie (1947-), English musician/actor
   ☐ Agree ☐ Disagree Why? ......................................................

7. "We did not change as we grew older; we just became more clearly ourselves."
   —Lynn Hall (1937-), prolific author of children's books
   ☐ Agree ☐ Disagree Why? ......................................................

8. "A foolish consistency is the hobgoblin of little minds."
   —Ralph Waldo Emerson (1803-1882), writer
   ☐ Agree ☐ Disagree Why? ......................................................

9. "To modernize is to adopt and to adapt, but it is also to re-create."
   —Octavio Paz (1914-1998), Mexican writer and diplomat
   ☐ Agree ☐ Disagree Why? ......................................................

10. "It is not the strongest of the species that survive, nor the most intelligent, but the one most responsive to change."
    —Charles Darwin (1809-1882), naturalist
    ☐ Agree ☐ Disagree Why? ......................................................

11. "Make change your friend."
    —Bill Clinton (1946-), 42nd U.S. President
    ☐ Agree ☐ Disagree Why? ......................................................

12. "A man needs a little madness, or else he never dares cut the rope and be free."
    —Nikos Kazantzakis (1883-1957), Greek writer, Nobel Prize winner
    ☐ Agree ☐ Disagree Why? ......................................................

13. "We must be the change we want to see in the world."
    —Gandhi (1869-1948), Indian statesman
    ☐ Agree ☐ Disagree Why? ......................................................

## ⭐ ON YOUR OWN

Before next class, choose a place which is special to you and write a few sentences about how it has changed since you were a child

43

# WATCHING OUR WORLD CHANGE

Have you heard about TED (Technology, Entertainment, Design) talks yet? These "riveting talks by remarkable people, free to the world." according to the TED.com website, come from global experts in many disciplines. The presenters give highly personal presentations that address many important and some fun topics in short, engaging talks. The exceptional pace of change—technological, social, and economic—remains a constant TED theme.

Give yourself time to explore the site, browsing by topic or speaker. Find a short video on a topic of particular interest to you that you can recommend. Watch it twice or more, answer the following questions, and be prepared to share your recommendation.

Title ................................................................................................................................................

Speaker ...........................................................................................................................................

Location ......................................................................................... Date .....................................


1. How did the presentation begin? ..................................................................................................
..........................................................................................................................................................

2. What is the theme of the talk? ....................................................................................................
..........................................................................................................................................................

3. What did you learn from this TED talk? ......................................................................................
..........................................................................................................................................................
..........................................................................................................................................................

4. What did the speaker want to accomplish? .................................................................................
..........................................................................................................................................................

5. What do you believe is the best thing about this TED talk? Why? ...............................................
..........................................................................................................................................................

6. How did the speaker connect to his audience? (Humor, visual aids, etc) ...................................
..........................................................................................................................................................

7. Did the speaker convince you? How? ...........................................................................................

8. Why did you choose this TED talk? ..............................................................................................
..........................................................................................................................................................

9. How would you rate this TED talk on a scale of 1-5? ..................................................................

10. Why are you recommending this particular talk to your classmates? .........................................
..........................................................................................................................................................

# CHAPTER 8

# HANDLING STRESS

## SHARING TIPS

Sometimes we all feel stressed. Take turns asking and responding to these questions. Feel free to skip any awkward questions. Listen sympathetically.

1. What are common reasons for stress in people's personal lives?

2. Have you felt stress recently? Describe a recent stressful experience.

3. Do you eat more or less when you're stressed? Do you have any special comfort foods?

4. Do your hands shake when you're stressed? Any other physical symptoms?

5. Do you know any "stress junkies" who thrive on pressure? What professions might attract these people? Why?

6. How can stress help you? Have you ever been inspired by stress?

7. Can stress be fun? Do you like horror movies? Do you like roller coasters? Are you a sports fan?

8. Have you ever been to a spa or had a massage? Did it help you relieve stress?

9. What kind of music relaxes you and relieves stress?

10. Do you exercise or play sports to lessen your stress? How often? Does it help?

## EXPANDING VOCABULARY

Circle the words that you already actively use. Review the other words.

| | | | | |
|---|---|---|---|---|
| stress | comfort | spa | unhealthy | roller-coaster |
| relieve | adventuresome | red flag | thrive | strive |

**stress** *noun*: pressure; mental or emotional strain from anxiety.

• She quit being an executive because it caused too much stress in her life.

**comfort**: *verb* to soothe or console; noun: ease, a relaxed state; lack of want, satisfaction.

• Rebecca is so grief-stricken I cannot comfort her.

**"There is more to life than increasing its speed."**

—Mahatma Gandhi (1869-1948), Indian statesman

46

**spa** *noun*: a resort or place to improve one's health; a hot tub or natural spring bath.

- Every winter his parents traveled to a spa for the steam room and mud baths.

**unhealthy** *adjective*: unwell, ill; not good for you, damaging.

- The air in the city today was considered unhealthy for children and the elderly.

**roller coaster** *noun*: a ride at an amusement park with cars traveling on narrow rails with sharp turns and bends.

- Lilly was too frightened to ride the roller coaster, but Dan loved it.

**relieve** *verb*: to ease; to reduce pain hunger or other discomfort or suffering.

- I usually take aspirin to relieve headaches.

**adventuresome** *adjective*: eager to discover or experience new or exciting things; willing to take risks.

- My Uncle Billy has an adventuresome spirit and hikes in places I'm afraid to go.

**red flag** *noun*: a warning sign.

- When my new friend yelled at his wife, it was a red flag for how he would treat me.

**thrive** *verb*: to grow, be successful, flourish.

- Now that the baby has better nutrition, she will thrive.

**strive** *verb*: to work toward a goal.

- The championship is something to strive for.

## PARAPHRASING PROVERBS, IDIOMS, AND PUNS

A. We have many expressions about stress. Read the following expressions, and discuss them with your partners. What do they mean? Circle your favorites. Explain your choices.

- Go with the flow. —American
- Worry often gives a small thing a big shadow. —Swedish
- Look before you leap. —American
- You can't catch the cubs without entering the tiger's den. —Korean
- Time spent laughing is time spent with the gods. —Japanese
- Smooth seas do not make skillful sailors. —English
- Bless, don't stress

B. Can you add two more proverbs about stress?

- ................................................................................................................

- ................................................................................................................

> "If I am not for myself, who will be for me? But if I am only for myself, what am I? And if not now, when?"
>
> —Hillel, (1st century CE), rabbi

1. Do you want relaxation, adventure, or something else from your vacation?

2. Does shopping reduce stress for you or does it create stress for you?

3. Can you name three unhealthy ways that people use to reduce stress?

4. Can you name three healthy ways that people use to reduce stress?

5. In which ways has the technology in your life reduced your stress?

6. In which ways has the technology in your life increased your stress?

7. Do you think you are more or less stressed than your parents were when they were the age you are now? In what ways? Why?

8. What are potential risks for people who seem to thrive on stress?

9. How do you know when you're stressed? Do you have a red flag warning?

10. How have you overcome stressful situations? How do you handle daily stress?

11. What stress-busting tips can you suggest for others?

12. Would you enjoy a stress-free life? Is it a possibility?

## DISCUSSING QUOTATIONS

Take turns reading these quotations out loud, and discuss them with your partners. Do you agree with the quotation? Disagree? Why? Mark your answer. Explain your response.

1. "There is no such thing as pure pleasure; some anxiety always goes with it."
   —Ovid (43 B.C. —18A.D.), poet
   ☐ Agree ☐ Disagree Why? ........................................................

2. "A problem is a chance for you to do your best."
   —Duke Ellington (1890-1974), jazz composer and band leader
   ☐ Agree ☐ Disagree Why? ........................................................

3. "The only thing we have to fear is fear itself."
   —Franklin Delano Roosevelt (1882-1945), 32nd U.S. President
   ☐ Agree ☐ Disagree Why? ........................................................

4. "Facing it-always facing it-that's the way you get through. Face it!"
   —Joseph Conrad (1857-1924), Polish-born British novelist
   ☐ Agree ☐ Disagree Why? ........................................................

5. "Don't sweat the small stuff, and it's all small stuff."
   —Dr. Richard Carlson (1956-), American author and psychologist
   ☐ Agree ☐ Disagree Why? ........................................................

6. "The chief danger in life is that you may take too many precautions."
   —Dr. Alfred Adler (1870-1937), Austrian psychologist
   ☐ Agree ☐ Disagree Why? ........................................................

7. "More than any time in history, mankind faces a crossroad: One path leads to despair and utter hopelessness; the other to total extinction. Let us pray we have the wisdom to choose correctly."
   —Woody Allen (1935-), American film director, actor, and comic
   ☐ Agree ☐ Disagree Why? ........................................................

8. "Man needs difficulties; they are necessary for health."
   —Carl Gustav Jung (1875-1961), Swiss psychiatrist
   ☐ Agree ☐ Disagree Why? ........................................................

9. "It was the best of times; it was the worst of times."
   —Charles Dickens (1812-1870), English novelist
   ☐ Agree ☐ Disagree Why? ........................................................

10. "Do what you can, with what you have, where you are."
    —Theodore Roosevelt (1858-1919), 26th U. S. President
    ☐ Agree ☐ Disagree Why? ........................................................

11. "I don't think of all the misery, but of the beauty that remains."
    —Anne Frank (1929-1945), writer
    ☐ Agree ☐ Disagree Why? ........................................................

12. "With me, a change of trouble is as good as a vacation."
    —David Lloyd George (1863-1945), British prime minister during WWI
    ☐ Agree ☐ Disagree Why? ........................................................

13. "In the depth of winter, I finally learned that within me there lay an invincible summer."
    —Albert Camus (1913-1960), French novelist
    ☐ Agree ☐ Disagree Why? ........................................................

14. "An early morning walk is a blessing for the whole day."
    —Henry David Thoreau (1817-1862), writer
    ☐ Agree ☐ Disagree Why? ........................................................

### ★ ON YOUR OWN

Find an article on dealing with stress. Prepare to share the information you found with your classmates in a small group. You might also be asked to give a very short report to the class.

**49**

# REDUCING STRESS AND INCREASING HAPPINESS

Student Name ..................................................................................................Class............................

Teacher ....................................................................................................... Date............................

We live in stressful times and often feel more stressed than blessed. How can we reduce our stress? How can we increase our happiness?

Take the five-minute online quiz called "How Happy Are You" that was featured on Oprah's popular talk show. The URL is http://apps.bluezones.com/happiness.

Answer the questions, read the evaluation, and be prepared to discuss stress management tips with your classmates.

1. What do you think of the quiz? Why? ......................................................................................

2. How many questions were asked? .................. 3. Can you recall two questions?

A. ...............................................................................................................................................

B. ...............................................................................................................................................

4. How would you rate the online quiz on a scale of 1-10? Why? .................................................


Now find a recent article on reducing stress and increasing happiness.

Title...........................................................................................................................................

Author:...................................................................................... Length...........................

Publication:.............................................................................. Publication date...........................

What's the main idea? ................................................................................................................
...................................................................................................................................................
...................................................................................................................................................

How many sources were quoted? ...............................................................................................

How credible were the sources quoted? Why? ...........................................................................
...................................................................................................................................................

How could the article be improved? Why? .................................................................................
...................................................................................................................................................
...................................................................................................................................................

On a scale of 1-10, how would you rate the article? Why?.........................................................
...................................................................................................................................................

# CHAPTER 9

# WORK RELATIONSHIPS

## SHARING STORIES

Most people have to work to survive. Some people love their work, and find their professions bring deep satisfaction. Many Americans, however, do what they must to pay their bills. What are your work experiences? Share your thoughts with your class partners. Remember to encourage each other as we prepare for successful careers.

1. Do you work? Are you retired?

2. Do you have a regular schedule? Which shift do you work?

3. Do you work alone or with other staff members?

4. Can you describe a typical day at work?

5. Do you use a computer at work? What computer software programs do you use?

6. Is there a career ladder at your workplace?

7. How do you get along with your co-workers? Are you a team player? Do you enjoy the work atmosphere?

8. Do you socialize with your co-workers outside of work? Where do you go?

9. How does your company/school encourage networking among co-workers?

10. Have you ever had a mentor? Who? How did this person teach you the ropes at work?

## EXPANDING VOCABULARY

Circle the words that you already actively use. Review the other words.

| | | | | |
|---|---|---|---|---|
| shift | title | retire | co-worker | profession |
| hire | fire | supervisor | mentor | ambition |

**shift** *noun*: a period of time one works, verb: to physically move or change position.

• The second shift at the hospital goes from 3 PM to 11 PM.

"Whether our work is art or science or the daily work of society, it is only the form in which we explore our experience which is different."

—Jacob Bronowski (1908-1974), scientist

**title** *noun*: the name of a book, movie, or work of art; a word that signifies a person's station in life or, such as Captain; or supervisor; a legal document that proves ownership.

• My boss has the title of director.

**retire** *verb*: to stop working, to end a career; to relax or go to sleep.

• Dr. Webb retired at age 70 after 40 years of teaching in the Engineering department.

**co-worker** *noun*: someone you work with; a peer on the job.

• Carolina was on the job longer than any of her co-workers.

**profession** *noun*: a career, a life's work.

• She's an engineer by profession, and she volunteers as a science tutor in our school.

**hire** *verb*: to employ, put someone on a job.

• Our research team needs to hire two more consultants.

**fire** *verb*: to dismiss someone from a job, to let go.

• My lab supervisor said she would fire me if I missed any more work.

**supervisor** *noun*: the boss; the person you report to on a job.

• Susan's supervisor pulled her aside to tell her she was doing a terrific job.

**mentor** *noun*: an experienced person; a teacher or wise person; one who provides guidance or training.

• Ralph was my mentor when I started my job at the post office.

**ambition** *noun*: a desire to be successful, drive; an aim or objective.

• Her secret ambition was to be vice-president.

## PARAPHRASING PROVERBS, IDIOMS, AND PUNS

A. We have many expressions about work. Read the following expressions, and discuss them with your partners. What do they mean? Circle your favorites. Explain your choices.

• Many hands make light work. —Latin
• Cash in hand is better than credit to a rich customer.—Korean
• Show, don't tell.
• Thank God it's Friday (TGIF)
• Too many pilots are bound to sink the ship. —Chinese
• All work and no play makes Jake a dull boy. —English
• Time is money. —Greek
• Work shall set you free.—German

B. Can you add two more proverbs about work?

- ......................................................................................................

- ......................................................................................................

1. Have you ever complained about a co-worker? A boss? How did they upset you?

2. How has a co-worker impressed you? What have you learned from your co-workers?

3. How is your profession shown in movies? Can you give an example?

4. What are some common misperceptions about your field? Example?

5. What qualities should a manager, director, or boss have in your field? Why?

6. What are some things a rude or obnoxious boss might do?

7. Have you ever had to deal with a rude, difficult, or crazy boss?

8. Who is the best manager, director, or boss you've ever had? Why?

9. Have you ever supervised someone? Were you a good manager? Why?

10. How would you describe your management style? Can you give an example?

11. Have you ever hired someone? What did you look for? Why?

12. Have you ever evaluated people at work? Have you had to fire someone? Why?

13. What makes someone a professional in your field? How can people stand out?

14. How do some people neglect their work duties because of family responsibilities?

15. Have you ever known someone to neglect their family because of work?

16. What is a workaholic?

17. How would you describe your work habits?

18. How do you keep track of your tasks, meetings, and relationships at work?

19. Do you have any time management tips to share?

20. Do you think most Americans work to live or live to work? Why?

21. Have you recently updated your professional skills? How?

22. What are your professional ambitions? Why?

Take turns reading these quotations out loud, and discuss them with your partners. Do you agree with the quotation? Disagree? Why? Mark your answer. Explain your response.

1. "Work keeps at bay three great evils: boredom, vice, and need."
   —Voltaire (1694-1778), French philosopher
   ☐ Agree ☐ Disagree Why? ........................................................

2. "I'm a great believer in luck, and I find the harder I work the more of it I have."
   —Thomas Jefferson (1743-1826), U.S. President and the man on the nickel
   ☐ Agree ☐ Disagree Why? ........................................................

3. "I don't like work—no man does—but I like what is in the work. The chance to find yourself."
   —Joseph Conrad (1857-1924), British novelist
   ☐ Agree ☐ Disagree Why? ........................................................

4. "Competition brings out the best in products and the worst in people."
   —David Sarnoff (1881-1971), leader of RCA
   ☐ Agree ☐ Disagree Why? ........................................................

5. "I don't meet competition; I crush it."
   —Charles Revson (1906-1975), founder of Revlon
   ☐ Agree ☐ Disagree Why? ........................................................

6. "Where work is a pleasure, life is a joy! When work is a duty, life is slavery."
   —Maxim Gorky (1868-1936), Russian/Soviet novelist
   ☐ Agree ☐ Disagree Why? ........................................................

7. "There are an enormous number of managers who have retired on the job."
   —Peter Drucker (1909-2005), American business guru
   ☐ Agree ☐ Disagree Why? ........................................................

8. "There is no such thing as a free lunch."
   —Milton Friedman (1912-2006), economist
   ☐ Agree ☐ Disagree Why? ........................................................

9. "Without work all life goes rotten."
   —Albert Camus (1913-1960), French writer
   ☐ Agree ☐ Disagree Why? ........................................................

10. "I'm lazy. But it's lazy people who invented the wheel and the bicycle because they didn't like walking or carrying things."
    —Lech Walesa (1943-), Polish President and Labor leader
    ☐ Agree ☐ Disagree Why? ........................................................

★ ON YOUR OWN

Choose a quote that relates to the job you have now or one you once had. In five sentences, tell the class how this quote relates to your work experience.

# CHAPTER 10
# PRACTICING JOB INTERVIEWS

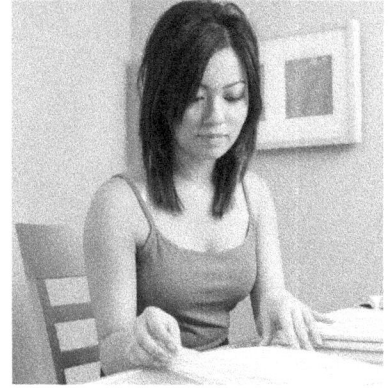

## ANTICIPATING QUESTIONS

Work with your partners and role-play applying for a position in your field. Switch roles every ten questions. Use complete sentences.

1. Have you ever worked in the United States before? Where?

2. Are you eligible to work in the U.S.? Can you provide documentation?

3. Have you ever been laid off? Have you ever been fired?

4. Have you ever been sued? Have you ever been arrested?

5. Have you ever taken a psychological test before?

6. Have you ever taken a lie detector test? A drug test? A handwriting test? A psychological test?

7. Have you ever quit without giving two weeks notice?

8. Have you ever studied computers? Have you worked with computers before?

## EXPANDING VOCABULARY

Circle the words that you already actively use. Review the other words.

| | | | | |
|---|---|---|---|---|
| apply | applicant | background | resign | bonus |
| misconduct | software | revoke | client | promoted |

**apply** *verb*: to make a written request; to use as a talent; to attach or coat such as to apply paint; to be relevant to something.

• I need to apply for unemployment compensation.

**applicant** *noun*: a person who applies for something.

• I hope I get the job but there dozens of other applicants.

**background** *noun*: facts about your personal history experience; upbringing; environment; a backdrop of scenery.

• Is there any writing experience in your background?

**resign** *verb*: to leave, or quit a job; to take an or to come to terms with something; (to be resigned to) to accept.

> **"Whenever you are asked if you can do a job, tell 'em, 'Certainly, I can!'— and get busy and find out how to do it."**
>
> —Theodore Roosevelt (1858-1919), cowboy, police chief, colonel, explorer, and 26th U.S. President

- Sally decided to resign rather than take a pay cut.

- I'm resigned to the fact I'll never be rich.

**bonus** *noun*: extra, like in payment for a job.

- At the end of the year, the company gave its hardest working assistants a bonus in their paychecks.

**misconduct** *noun*: bad behavior; breaking the rules.

- The coach will not tolerate any misconduct on the part of his players, no matter how talented they are.

**software** *noun*: a computer program or application.

- Steve Jobs dropped out of college and created computers that changed the world.

**client** *noun*: someone you give professional service to, a customer of a professional such as an attorney.

- She's a successful attorney with many clients.

**promoted** *adjective*: having achieved a higher station; verb: to have elevated or to have publicized.

- Raj was promoted at work after only a few weeks.

### PARAPHRASING PROVERBS, IDIOMS, AND PUNS

A. We have many expressions about speaking and work. Read the following expressions, and discuss them with your partners. What do they mean? Circle your favorites. Explain your choices.

- Think before you speak.

- The secret of getting ahead is getting started.

- Short answers save trouble.

- What you don't ask for, you don't get.

- Silence can speak volumes.

- Silence equals consent.

- Know your audience.

- Praise is always pleasing.

- Anything worth having is worth working for.

B. Can you add two more proverbs about work or speaking?

- ................................................................................................................

- ................................................................................................................

1. What did you learn from your last job? Best manager? Worst boss?

2. Have you ever been certified in a professional field? How did you prepare?

3. Have you ever been evaluated by a supervisor? What did you learn?

4. What suggestions have you made at work to help the company?

5. Were your suggestions adopted? Were the suggestions successful?

6. Have you ever been promoted? What was your new title?

7. Have you ever received a bonus? Have you ever gotten a raise?

8. Have you ever worked on commission? Have you ever worked as a salesperson?

9. Have you ever traveled out of town for work? What did you do?

10. Have you ever volunteered for overtime? Have you ever declined overtime?

11. Have you ever worked on the weekends? Week nights?

12. Have you ever worked 12-hour shifts? What shift is best for you?

13. Have you ever spoken English with customers or clients?

14. Have you ever worked as a mechanic/salesperson/researcher/nurse?

15. Have you ever taken care of young children? In America?

16. Do you prefer working alone or with others? Why?

17. What items have you sold? Did you sell merchandise in English?

18. Have you ever worked with difficult customers? What was your approach? Did it work?

19. Have you ever hired people? What did you look for in applicants?

20. Have you ever worked as a supervisor? Foreman? Manager?

21. What tips do you have for young people entering your profession?

22. Why should you be hired for this position?

## DISCUSSING QUOTATIONS

Take turns reading these quotations out loud, and discuss them with your partners. Do you agree with the quotation? Disagree? Why? Mark your answer. Explain your response.

1. "The difference between a job and a career is the difference between 40 and 60 hours a week."
   —Robert Frost (1874-1963), poet
   ☐ Agree ☐ Disagree Why? .............................................................

2. "You have to have your heart in the business and the business in your heart."
   —Thomas J. Watson (1874-1956), founder of IBM
   ☐ Agree ☐ Disagree Why? ....................................................

3. "If you don't know where you are going, you will probably end up somewhere else."
   —Dr. Laurence J. Peter (1919-1990 ), educator
   ☐ Agree ☐ Disagree Why? ....................................................

4. "In a hierarchy every employee tends to rise to his level of incompetence."
   —Dr. Laurence J. Peter (1919-1990), educator
   ☐ Agree ☐ Disagree Why? ....................................................

5. "You may be disappointed if you fail, but you are doomed if you don't try."
   —Beverly Sills (1929-2007), opera singer
   ☐ Agree ☐ Disagree Why? ....................................................

6. "Luck is not something that you can mention in the presence of self-made men."
   —E.B. White (1899-1985), American writer
   ☐ Agree ☐ Disagree Why? ....................................................

7. "In business for yourself, not by yourself."
   —Ray Kroc (1902-1984), McDonald's founder
   ☐ Agree ☐ Disagree Why? ....................................................

8. My father taught me to work; he did not teach me to love it."
   —Abraham Lincoln (1809-1865), 16th U.S. President
   ☐ Agree ☐ Disagree Why? ....................................................

9. "I want to work for a company that contributes to and is part of a community. I want not just to invest in; I want to believe in."
   —Anita Roddick (1943-2007), Body Shop founder
   ☐ Agree ☐ Disagree Why? ....................................................

10. "The only place where success comes before work is in the dictionary."
    —Vidal Sassoon (1928-), hair stylist and salon tycoon
    ☐ Agree ☐ Disagree Why? ....................................................

11. "If you have to support yourself, you had bloody well better find some way that is going to be interesting. And you don't do that by sitting around."
    —Katharine Hepburn (1907-2003), movie icon
    ☐ Agree ☐ Disagree Why? ....................................................

12. "Success is 10 percent inspiration and 90 percent perspiration."
    —Thomas A. Edison (1847-1931), American inventor
    ☐ Agree ☐ Disagree Why? ....................................................

⭐ ON YOUR OWN

You have started a new business. How will you choose your employees? List the first seven steps you will take.

1. ....................................................

2. ....................................................

3. ....................................................

4. ....................................................

5. ....................................................

6. ....................................................

7. ....................................................

# FINDING ADVICE ON JOB INTERVIEW TECHNIQUES

Student Name ....................................................................................................................Class............................

Teacher .................................................................................................................. Date.........................

Please find a YouTube videoclip that helps people successfully interview for jobs— in English—that you would like to share with your classmates.

Watch the video, take notes, and review it for your classmates.

1. Video title ..............................................................................................................................................

2. Web address................................................................................................. 3. Length............................

4. Creator ..................................................................................................................................................

5. Please describe the video...........................................................................................................................

..................................................................................................................................................................

..................................................................................................................................................................

6. What interview tips did the video provide? ...................................................................................................

..................................................................................................................................................................

7. Where do you think the video was produced? Why? .......................................................................................

..................................................................................................................................................................

8. How practical did you find the advice? Why? ...............................................................................................

..................................................................................................................................................................

9. What was the strongest part? Why?.............................................................................................................

..................................................................................................................................................................

10. What was the weakest part? Why? .............................................................................................................

..................................................................................................................................................................

11. Who do think is the target audience for this video? .......................................................................................

..................................................................................................................................................................

12. Why did you choose this video?.................................................................................................................

..................................................................................................................................................................

13. How would you rate this video on a scale of 1-5? Why? ...............................................................................

..................................................................................................................................................................

**www.CompellingConversations.com**

# CHAPTER 11

# VOTING AND CHOOSING LEADERS

## SHARING VIEWS

Voting and having your vote count remain rare privileges around the world. Discuss elections and issues with your partners.

1. Does your native country have elections? How often?

2. Can women vote? What's the minimum age? Can religious minorities vote?

3. Where do people physically vote? How do voters mark their ballots?

4. Do the candidates campaign? How?

5. Do the candidates hold televised debates? Who asks the questions?

6. Can you recall any political ads from a campaign?

7. What were some important issues in the last election?

8. Can you compare and contrast elections here with those in your native country?

## EXPANDING VOCABULARY

Circle the words that you already actively use. Review the other words.

| | | | | |
|---|---|---|---|---|
| candidate | absentee | campaign | debates | contrast |
| election | eligible | participate | recall | referendum |
| apathy | polls | | | |

**candidate** *noun*: someone running for political office; someone being considered for a job.

• Carmen seemed like the perfect candidate for the position until we interviewed Diana.

**absentee** *noun*: someone not present.
**absentee** *adjective* describing something or someone not physically present.

• Wang wasn't in school so he was counted among the absentees.

• Min voted by absentee ballot.

**"If ever there was a doubt about the importance of exercising the most fundamental right of citizenship, it was clearly answered by the first presidential election of the 21st century."**

—Bill Clinton (1946-) 42nd U.S. President

**campaign** *noun*: the events leading up to a vote in an election; a movement or struggle to achieve something.

• In many countries, election campaigns last only six weeks. In the United States they last longer than six months.

**participate** *verb*: to be involved in, to act or take part in.

• This year six political parties will participate in the election.

**debate** *noun*: a formal discussion or argument over issues; a back-and-forth discussion between two sides.
**debate** *verb*: to argue; to ponder something carefully.

• The candidates agreed to hold three debates that would be televised across the nation.

• We debated all night, and became closer friends.

**contrast** *noun*: a difference, distinction.
**contrast** *verb*: to compare different things.

• His quiet voice stood in contrast to his forceful ideas.

• Shi loves black-and-white photography because of the contrast between shades of gray.

**election** *noun*: the process of people voting, selecting among candidates for office.

• Brazil held elections last month.

**eligible** *adjective*: qualified for, entitled to, permitted.

• Once you are 18 years old, you are eligible to vote in the United States.

**recall** *verb*: to remember; to revoke or cancel; vote to remove someone from office.

• People wanted to recall the governor because he broke his campaign promises.

**referendum**: a vote put to everyone.

• They announced that a referendum on the new tax proposal would be held in June.

**apathy** *noun*: a lack of interest, indifference, not caring.

• The voters showed apathy by not showing up to vote on the referendum.

**polls**: *noun* the places people go to vote; surveys taken by experts to find out how people feel about candidates or topics.

• I didn't have to wait long at the polls to vote.

## PARAPHRASING PROVERBS, IDIOMS, AND PUNS

A. We have many expressions about elections. Read the following expressions, and discuss them with your partners. What do they mean? Circle your favorites. Explain your choices.

- To the victor belong the spoils.
- The squeaky wheel gets the grease.
- Who rules whom?
- Stand up and be counted.
- A week is a long time in politics.
- Counting votes counts more than voting

B. Can you add two more proverbs about politics?

- ........................................................................................................
- ........................................................................................................

## THE CONVERSATION CONTINUES

1. Have you ever voted in an American election?

2. What are some advantages to the American system? Disadvantages?

3. What are referendums or initiatives? Can citizens in your state vote directly on reforms?

4. What is a public bond? What do government bonds finance?

5. Do voters have the right to recall public officials in your state?

6. What makes an effective or strong candidate? Why?

7. Who is the President? Who is the Vice President? To what party do they belong?

8. Who are your state's Senators? Who is your Congressional Representative?

9. Who is the governor of your state? The mayor of your city?

10. What are some qualities you look for in elected officials? Why?

11. Who are some significant political leaders in the world today? Why did you select those leaders?

12. What are the advantages of being a naturalized citizen?

13. What are some important issues in your state right now? Why?

14. What are some local issues in your neighborhood or city? Why?

15. What do you think are some important national issues? Why?

16. What is apathy? Why is apathy so common among voters?

17. How could the election system be improved?

18. Do you expect to vote in the next election? Why?

## DISCUSSING QUOTATIONS

Take turns reading these quotations out loud, and discuss them with your partners. Do you agree with the quotation? Disagree? Why? Mark your answer. Explain your response.

1. "Always do the right thing. This will gratify some and astonish the rest."
   —Mark Twain (1835-1910), American humorist
   ☐ Agree ☐ Disagree Why? .....................................................

2. "...government of the people, by the people, for the people shall not perish from the earth."
   —Abraham Lincoln (1809-1865), 16th U.S. President
   ☐ Agree ☐ Disagree Why? .....................................................

3. "This woman's place is in the House—the House of Representatives."
   —Bella Abzug (1920-1998), American Congresswomen and feminist
   ☐ Agree ☐ Disagree Why? .....................................................

4. "The only thing necessary for the triumph of evil is for good men to do nothing."
   —Edmund Burke (1729-1797), English statesman
   ☐ Agree ☐ Disagree Why? .....................................................

5. "Sometimes it is said that man cannot be trusted with the government of himself. Can he, then, be trusted with the government of others?"
   —Thomas Jefferson (1743-1826), U.S. President
   ☐ Agree ☐ Disagree Why? .....................................................

6. "Where annual elections end, there slavery begins."
   —John Adams (1735-1826), 2nd U.S. President
   ☐ Agree ☐ Disagree Why? .....................................................

7. "Elections are won by men and women chiefly because most people vote against somebody rather than for somebody."
   —Franklin Pierce Adams (1881-1960), journalist
   ☐ Agree ☐ Disagree Why? .....................................................

8. "If the Republicans will stop telling lies about the Democrats, we will stop telling the truth about them."
   —Adlai Stevenson (1900-1965), American statesman
   ☐ Agree ☐ Disagree Why? .....................................................

9. "I belong to no organized political party—I am a Democrat."
   —Will Rogers (1879-1935), American humorist and columnist
   ☐ Agree ☐ Disagree Why? .....................................................

10. "I would rather be right than be President."
    —Henry Clay (1777-1852), U.S. politician
    ☐ Agree ☐ Disagree Why? ........................................................

11. "Democracy is the worst system devised by the wit of man except for all the others."
    —Winston Churchill (1874-1965 ), British Prime Minister
    ☐ Agree ☐ Disagree Why? ........................................................

12. "An election cannot give a country a firm sense of direction if it has two or more national parties which merely have different names, but are as alike in their principles and aims as two peas in the same pod."
    —Franklin D. Roosevelt (1882-1945), 32nd U.S. President; elected four times
    ☐ Agree ☐ Disagree Why? ........................................................

13. "The happy ending is our national belief."
    —Mary McCarthy (1912-1989), American novelist and critic
    ☐ Agree ☐ Disagree Why? ........................................................

## ⭐ ON YOUR OWN

Create five campaign slogans for a candidate or cause of your choice.

1. ........................................................
........................................................

2. ........................................................
........................................................

3. ........................................................
........................................................

4. ........................................................
........................................................

5. ........................................................
........................................................

# FOLLOWING POLITICAL NEWS

Student Name ...........................................................................................................Class...........................

Teacher ..................................................................................................... Date...........................

What political issue matters to you? What political news are you following? Find a recent article (500-1,000 words) about an important issue or political event in the news. Clip the article, and bring it to class to discuss with your classmates.

Title...................................................................................................................................................

Author:..................................................................................................Length...........................

Publication:.................................................................................. Publication date...........................

Topic.................................................................................................................................................

..........................................................................................................................................................

What's the main idea? ........................................................................................................................

..........................................................................................................................................................

..........................................................................................................................................................

How many sources were quoted? .......................................................................................................

How credible were the sources quoted? Why? ...................................................................................

..........................................................................................................................................................

..........................................................................................................................................................

What kind of political issue does the article describe?.......................................................................

..........................................................................................................................................................

..........................................................................................................................................................

Who does this issue directly concern? Why? .....................................................................................

..........................................................................................................................................................

..........................................................................................................................................................

Who is indirectly touched by this change? Why? ..............................................................................

..........................................................................................................................................................

..........................................................................................................................................................

Why did you choose this article?........................................................................................................

..........................................................................................................................................................

..........................................................................................................................................................

**"All's well that ends well."**
William Shakespeare
(1564–1616), playwright and poet

# TO ENGLISH STUDENTS AND TEACHERS

We want you to speak as much English as possible, both in and outside of your English classes here in the United States and back home in your native country. These extra materials can be used to deepen the classroom experience, for homework, or for self-study. These bonus materials are optional and supplemental—but clearly recommended.

Time restrictions and class sizes often limit the use of these supplemental activities. Many chapters include opportunities for students to give brief presentations. Feedback is helpful so we can learn what our audience heard and thought. Therefore, we have included forms for both instructor and peer feedback. We believe peer feedback forms provide valuable information. It's also considered a recommended "best practice" in many American classrooms because the entire audience can ask questions and share ideas. The goal is to create a more democratic atmosphere in the English classroom.

The Academic Word list is highly recommended if you plan to take the TOEFL or IELTS exams. The vocabulary will also help prepare students who want to work for international business companies or plan to take the TOEIC exam.

We want to share these bonus worksheets so you can continually improve your English and create your own compelling conversations both inside and outside the classroom.

- Student Presentation: Instructor Evaluation
- Student Presentation: Peer Response and a Question
- Student Presentation: Self-Evaluation
- Reviewing More Pronunciation Tips on the Internet
- The Academic Word List

# STUDENT PRESENTATION: INSTRUCTOR EVALUATION

1. Speaker:....................................................................................................................................................

2. Topic:.......................................................................................................................................................

3. Date: .........................................................................................................4. Time.............................

5. What was good to see in their presentation?.......................................................................................

....................................................................................................................................................................

....................................................................................................................................................................

....................................................................................................................................................................

....................................................................................................................................................................

6. What could have been better? What still needs to be improved? ......................................................

....................................................................................................................................................................

....................................................................................................................................................................

....................................................................................................................................................................

....................................................................................................................................................................

7. Other observations and tips: ..............................................................................................................

....................................................................................................................................................................

....................................................................................................................................................................

....................................................................................................................................................................

....................................................................................................................................................................

8. Two tips for the student to improve their English speaking skills:

- ...............................................................................................................................................................

....................................................................................................................................................................

....................................................................................................................................................................

....................................................................................................................................................................

- ...............................................................................................................................................................

....................................................................................................................................................................

....................................................................................................................................................................

....................................................................................................................................................................

# STUDENT PRESENTATION: PEER RESPONSE AND A QUESTION

Please provide feedback to your classmates on their presentations.

1. Speaker:.................................................................................................................................

2. Topic:...............................................................................................3. Date...........................

4. What was good to see in this presentation?.........................................................................

..................................................................................................................................................

..................................................................................................................................................

..................................................................................................................................................

..................................................................................................................................................

..................................................................................................................................................

..................................................................................................................................................

..................................................................................................................................................

5. What could have been better? What still needs to be improved? .......................................

..................................................................................................................................................

..................................................................................................................................................

..................................................................................................................................................

..................................................................................................................................................

..................................................................................................................................................

..................................................................................................................................................

6. Please share some other observations and tips about the speaker or topic. ......................

..................................................................................................................................................

..................................................................................................................................................

..................................................................................................................................................

..................................................................................................................................................

..................................................................................................................................................

..................................................................................................................................................

7. Please write a question to ask the speaker about the topic.................................................

..................................................................................................................................................

# STUDENT PRESENTATION: SELF-EVALUATION

1. Speaker:................................................................................................................................

2. Topic:.................................................................................................................................

3. Date ....................................................................................4. Time:................................

5. What was good to see in your presentation? ...........................................................................

................................................................................................................................................

................................................................................................................................................

................................................................................................................................................

................................................................................................................................................

................................................................................................................................................

6. What could have been better? What still needs to be improved? ...............................................

................................................................................................................................................

................................................................................................................................................

................................................................................................................................................

................................................................................................................................................

7. Other observations and tips: .................................................................................................

................................................................................................................................................

................................................................................................................................................

................................................................................................................................................

8. What are two things that you will improve on your next presentation?

- •	...................................................................................................................................

................................................................................................................................................

................................................................................................................................................

- •	...................................................................................................................................

................................................................................................................................................

................................................................................................................................................

# REVIEWING PRONUNCIATION TIPS ON THE INTERNET

Student Name .............................................................................................Class.............................

Teacher .......................................................................................... Date................................

Please find another video on the Internet that reviews English pronunciation that you would like to share. Watch the video, carefully listen, take notes, and practice.

1. Video title: ..........................................................................................................................

2. Web address:.........................................................................3. Length...............................

4. Creator: ..............................................................................................................................

5. Please describe the video: ....................................................................................................

...............................................................................................................................................

...............................................................................................................................................

6. What pronunciation tips did the video provide?...................................................................

...............................................................................................................................................

...............................................................................................................................................

7. Which words or sounds did the video focus on?...................................................................

...............................................................................................................................................

8. How practical did you find the advice? Why? .....................................................................

...............................................................................................................................................

9. What was the strongest part? Why?.....................................................................................

...............................................................................................................................................

...............................................................................................................................................

10. What was the weakest part? Why? .....................................................................................

...............................................................................................................................................

...............................................................................................................................................

11. Who do think is the target audience for this video? ...........................................................

12. Why did you choose this video? .........................................................................................

...............................................................................................................................................

13. How would you rate this video on a 1-to-5 scale? Why?.....................................................

# THE ACADEMIC WORD LIST

What is the Academic Word List? Why does it matter? How can it help you get a higher TOEFL Score?

Let's start with what many ambitious students hoping to go to college or study abroad already know. TOEFL scores count and focusing on the Academic Word List (AWL) helps students score higher on the TOEFL—across the curriculum.

English teachers naturally notice and appreciate a strong vocabulary, and academic writing requires a more formal register than casual oral speech. Standardized tests also reward a rich vocabulary and often explicitly test vocabulary skills. Nuance and precision can also be displayed by finding the appropriate word. Therefore, English language learners naturally seek to develop a strong academic vocabulary in order to succeed as college and university students.

Yet what are the key words that a college student needs for academic success in English? Professor Averil Coxhead at the School of Linguistics and Applied Language Studies at Victoria University of Wellington, New Zealand studied a wide range of academic texts across disciplines in the late 1990s. He culled 570 word families that he deemed vital for college preparation and created the Academic Word

List. The list was further divided into 10 sub-lists, from the most frequent to the least frequent. (We've alphabetized the 10 sub-sets to easily look up words in the dictionary.)

Because of Coxhead's systematic approach and the clear need for this type of focused vocabulary list to help determined, focused college bound international students, the AWL quickly established itself within academic high schools around the world. Many intensive English programs also adopted the AWL for their college prep programs, creating a niche within the English language classrooms. Although an intense controversy has arisen over the extensive focus on this vocabulary list, motivated students (like you!) should become at least familiar with the AWL.

Let's begin with better English conversations in our English classrooms. Adding more AWL words and teaching explicit vocabulary enrichment exercises— in your writing and speaking—is a simple, effective method. Please pay extra attention to these words in your academic courses.

Here for your reading pleasure and further study is the entire AWL in ten subsections.

### SUBLIST 1

| | | | |
|---|---|---|---|
| analysis | create | function | percent | source |
| approach | data | identified | period | specific |
| area | definition | income | policy | structure |
| assessment | derived | indicate | principle | theory |
| assume | distribution | individual | procedure | variables |
| authority | economic | interpretation | process | |
| available | environment | involved | required | **SUBLIST 2** |
| benefit | established | issues | research | achieve |
| concept | estimate | labour | response | acquisition |
| consistent | evidence | legal | role | administration |
| constitutional | expert | legislation | section | affect |
| context | factors | major | sector | appropriate |
| contract | financial | method | significant | aspects |
| | formula | occur | similar | assistance |

categories
chapter
commission
community
complex
computer
conclusion
conduct
construction
consequences
consumer
credit
cultural
design
distinction
elements
equation
evaluation
features
final
focus
impact
injury
institute
investment
items
journal
maintenance
normal
obtained
participation
perceived
positive
potential
previous
primary

purchase
range
region
regulations
relevant
resident
resources
restricted
security
select
site
sought
strategies
survey
text
tradition
transfer

### SUBLIST 3
alternative
circumstance
comments
compensation
component
consent
considerable
constant
constraints
contribution
convention
coordination
core
corporate
corresponding
criteria
deduction
demonstrate

dominant
document
emphasis
ensure
excluded
framework
funds
illustrated
immigration
implies
initial
instance
interaction
justification
layer
link
location
maximum
minorities
negative
outcomes
partnership
philosophy
physical
proportion
published
reaction

registered
reliance
removed
scheme
sequence
sex
shift
specified

sufficient
task
technical
techniques
technology
validity
volume

### SUBLIST 4
access
adequate
annual
apparent
approximate
attitudes
attributed
civil
code
communication
commitment
concentration
conference
contrast
cycle
debate
despite
dimensions
domestic
emerged
error
ethnic
goals
granted
hence
hypothesis
implementation
implications

imposed
integration
internal
investigation
job
label
mechanism
obvious
occupational
option
output
overall
parallel
parameters
phase
predicted
principal
prior
professional
project
promote
regime
resolution
retained
series
statistics
status
stress
subsequent
sum
summary
undertaken

### SUBLIST 5
academic
adjustment
alter

amendment
aware
capacity
challenge
clause
compounds
conflict
consultation
contact
decline
draft
discretion
equivalent
enable
energy
enforcement
entities
evolution
expansion
exposure
external
facilitate
fundamental
generated
generation
image
liberal
license
logic
marginal
medical
mental
modified
monitoring
network
notion

objective
orientation
perspective
precise
prime
psychology
pursue
ratio
rejected
revenue
stability
styles
substitute
sustainable
symbolic
target
transition
trend
version
welfare
whereas
monitoring

## SUBLIST 6
abstract
accurate
acknowledged
aggregate
allocation
assigned
attached
author
bond
brief
capable
cited
cooperative

discrimination
display
diversity
domain
edition
enhanced
estate
exceed
expert
explicit
federal
fees
flexibility
furthermore
gender
ignored
incentive
incidence
incorporated
index
inhibition
initiatives
input
instructions
intelligence
interval
lecture
migration
minimum
ministry
motivation
neutral
nevertheless
overseas
preceding
presumption

rational
recovery
revealed
scope
subsidiary
tapes
trace
transformation
transport
underlying
utility

## SUBLIST 7
adaptation
adults
advocate
aid
channel
chemical
classical
comprehensive
comprise
confirmed
converted
contrary
couple
decades
definite
deny
differentiation
disposal
dynamic
eliminate
empirical
equipment
extract
file

finite
foundation
global
grade
guarantee
hierarchical
identical
ideology
inferred
innovation
insert
intervention
isolated
media
mode
paradigm
phenomenon
priority
prohibited
publication
quotation
release
reverse
simulation
solely
somewhat
submitted
successive
survive
thesis
topic
transmission
ultimately
unique
visible
voluntary

abandon
accompany
accumulation
ambiguous
appendix
appreciation
arbitrary
automatically
bias
chart
clarity
commodity
complement
conformity
contemporary
contradiction
crucial
currency
denote
detected
deviation
displacement
dramatic
eventually
exhibit
exploitation
fluctuations
guidelines
highlighted
implicit
induced
inevitably
infrastructure

inspection
intensity
manipulation
minimizes
nuclear
offset
paragraph
plus
practitioners
predominantly
prospect
radical
random
reinforced
restore
revision
schedule
tension
termination
theme
thereby
uniform
vehicle
via
virtually
visual
widespread

## SUBLIST 9

accommodation
analogous
anticipated
assurance
attained

bulk
behalf
ceases
coherence
coincide
commenced
concurrent
confined
controversy
conversely
concurrent
device
devoted
diminished
distorted
duration
ethical
erosion
format
founded
incompatible
inherent
insights
integral
intermediate
manual
mature
mediation
military
minimal
mutual
norms

overlap
passive
portion
preliminary
protocol
qualitative
refine
relaxed
restraints
revolution
rigid
route
scenario
sphere
subordinate
supplementary
suspended
team
temporary
trigger
unified
vision
violation

## SUBLIST 10

adjacent
albeit
assembly
collapse
colleagues
compiled
conceived

convinced
depression
encountered
enormous
forthcoming
inclination
integrity
intrinsic
invoked
levy
likewise
nonetheless
notwithstanding
odd
ongoing
panel
persistent
posed
reluctant
so-called
straightforward
undergo
whereby

---

*Source: Wikitionary – Academic Word List accessed on 2/15/09 and alphabetized on 6/22/10.*

# BIBLIOGRAPHY

21st Century Dictionary of Quotations. Dell Publishing, 1993.

Ackerman, Mary Alice. Conversations on the Go. Search Institute, 2004.

Akbar, Fatollah. The Eye of an Ant: Persian Proverbs and Poems. Iranbooks, 1995.

Ben Shea, Noah. Great Jewish Quotes: Five Thousand Years of Truth and Humor from the Bible to George Burns. Ballantine Books, 1993.

Berman, Louis A. Proverb Wit and Wisdom: A Treasury of Proverbs, Parodies, Quips, Quotes, Cliches, Catchwords, Epigrams, and Aphorisms. Perigee Book, 1997.

Bierce, Ambrose. The Devil's Dictionary. Dover Publications, 1993.

Bullivant, Alison. The Little Book of Humorous Quotations. Barnes & Noble Books, 2002.

Byrne, Robert. 1,911 Best Things Anybody Ever Said. Ballantine Books, 1988.

Cohen, M. J. The Penguin Dictionary of Epigrams. Penguin, 2001.

Esar, Evan. 20,000 Quips and Quotes. Barnes & Noble Books. 1995.

Frank, Leonard Roy. Freedom: Quotes and Passages from the World's Greatest Freethinkers. Random House, 2003.

Galef, David. Even Monkeys Fall From Trees: The Wit and Wisdom of Japanese Proverbs. Tuttle Publishing, 1987.

Galef, David. Even a Stone Buddha Can Talk: More Wit and Wisdom of Japanese Proverbs. Tuttle Publishing, 2000.

Gross, David C. and Gross, Esther R. Jewish Wisdom: A Treasury of Proverbs, Maxims, Aphorisms, Wise Sayings, and Memorable Quotations. Walker and Company, 1992.

Gross, John. The Oxford Book of Aphorisms. Oxford University Press, 1987.

Habibian, Simin K. 1001 Persian-English Proverbs: Learning Language and Culture Through Commonly Used Sayings. Third Edition. Ibex Publishers, 2002.

Jacobs, Ben and Hjalmarsson, Helena. The Quotable Book Lover. Barnes & Noble, 2002.

Jarski, Rosemarie. Wisecracks: Great Lines from the Classic Hollywood Era. Contemporary Books, 1999.

Lewis, Edward and Myers, Robert. A Treasury of Mark Twain: The Greatest Humor of the Greatest American Humorist. Hallmark Cards, 1967.

McLellan, Vern. Quips, Quotes, and Quests. Harvest Books, 1982.

MacHale, Des. Wit. Andrews McMeel Publishing, 2003.

McWilliams, Peter. Life 101: Everything We Wish We Had Learned About Life In School - But Didn't. Prelude Press, 1991.

The Oxford Dictionary of Quotations, 5th Edition. Oxford University Press, 1999.

Peter, Dr. Laurence J. Peter's Quotations: Ideas for Our Time. William Morrow, 1977.

Pickney, Maggie. Pocket Positives For Our Times. The Five Mile Press, 2002.

Pickney, Maggie. The Devil's Collection: A Cynic's Dictionary. The Five Mile Press, 2003.

Platt, Suzy. Respectfully Quoted: A Dictionary of Quotations. Barnes & Noble Books, 1993.

Poole, Garry. The Complete Book of Questions. Willow-Creek Association, 2003.

Rado, Adam. Conversation Pieces. Aethron Press. 2001.

Reader's Digest Quotable Quotes: Wit and Wisdom for All Occasions From America's Most Popular Magazine. Reader's Digest, 1997

Rosten, Leo. Rome Wasn't Burned in a Day; The Mischief of Language. Doubleday, 1972.

Rosten, Leo. Leo Rosten's Carnival of Wit. Penguin Books USA, 1994.

Shalit, Gene. Great Hollywood Wit: A Glorious Cavalcade of Hollywood Wisecracks, Zingers, Japes, Quips, Slings, Jests, Snappers, and Sass from the Stars. St. Martin's Griffin, 2002

Simpson, James Beasley. Best Quotes of '54, '55, '56. Thomas Y. Crowell Company, 1957.

Stavropoulos, Steven. The Wisdom of the Ancient Greeks: Timeless Advice on the Senses, Society, and the Soul. Barnes & Noble Books, 2003.

Sullivan, George. Quotable Hollywood. Barnes and Noble, 2001.

Webster's Dictionary of Quotations. Merriam-Webster, 1992.

Williams, Rose. Latin Quips at Your Fingertips: Witty Latin Sayings by Wise Romans. Barnes and Noble, 2000.

Winokur, Jon. The Portable Curmudgeon. Jon. New American Library, 1987.

Winkour, Jon. Zen to Go. New American Library, 1989.

Winkour, Jon. The Traveling Curmudgeon. Sasquatch Books, 2003.

Yong-chol, Kim. Proverbs East and West: An Anthology of Chinese, Korean, and Japanese Saying with Western Equivalents. Hollym, 1991.

Zubko, Andy. Treasury of Spiritual Wisdom: A Collection of 10,000 Inspirational Quotations. Blue Dove Press.1996.

The internet has dramatically expanded our access to quotations. Five websites deserve to be mentioned here as outstanding sources.

- www.bartleby.com/quotations
- www.qotd.org
- www.quotationspage.com
- www.thinkexist.com
- http://en.wikiquote.org

# ABOUT THE AUTHORS

## ERIC H. ROTH

Eric H. Roth teaches international graduate students the pleasures and perils of academic writing and public speaking in English at the University of Southern California (USC). He also consults English language schools on communicative methods to effectively teach English in the United States and Vietnam.

Given a full scholarship as a Lilly Scholar, Roth studied philosophy and American history at Wabash College (1980-1984), and received his M.A. in Media Studies from the New School (1988). Since 1992, Roth has taught English to high school, community college, adult, and university students. Highlights of his career include: teaching the first Saturday morning citizenship class in Santa Monica 1994); directing the CES Adult Education Center (1995-1998); teaching at UCLA Extension (1997-2000, 2003-2005); teaching USC engineering students in Madrid, Spain (2007) and Paris, France (2008); and directing the APU International High School in Ho Chi Minh City, Vietnam (2009).

Roth co-authored *Compelling Conversations: Questions and Quotations on Timeless Topics* in 2006 to help English language learners increase their English fluency.

Recommended by English Teaching Professional magazine, the advanced ESL textbook has been used in over 40 countries in English classrooms and conversation clubs. Easy English Times, an adult literacy newspaper, has published a monthly column, "Instant Conversation Activities," based on the book since 2008. The first specific version for a particular country, Vietnam, was published in 2011. Future versions for Japan, Korea, Israel, Mexico, and Romania are anticipated.

A member of the USC faculty since 2003, Roth is a member of numerous professional organizations including: California Association of Teaching English to Speakers of Other Languages (CATESOL); the International Communication Association (ICA); the International Professors Project (IPP); and Teaching English to Speakers of Other Languages (TESOL). Roth has given several CATESOL conference presentations and led many teacher training workshops.

## TONI ABERSON

After 35 years of teaching English and supervising English teachers, Toni Aberson (M.A. English; M.A. Psychology and Religion) believes that a dynamic classroom is the optimal learning environment. She has taught English to high school students, adult refugees, and university scholars in New York, Indiana, and North Carolina.

"The key in a classroom is engagement," notes Aberson, "and people become interested and excited when they're learning about the daily stuff of life. When they are thinking and writing and talking about their real lives—food, jobs, family, friends, homes, sports, movies—that's when they learn the language."

"Learning English is not easy," continues Aberson, "but it can also be fun and stimulating. The fun comes English students realize its safe to say what they really feel and think—not what somebody told them they were supposed to feel. Give students permission to be themselves. Then students want to learn the right English words to tell their own life stories in their own words."

"Adult English students bring a wealth of interesting experiences with them," observes Aberson. "They bring the world into the classroom. The challenge for English teachers is to put students at ease and encourage learners to practice English. What better way than to ask students about their lives and beliefs? *Compelling Conversations* makes this challenge a bit easier for English teachers and tutors."

Aberson has launched a new Chimayo Press series for ESL students. *Lively ESL Lessons: American Idioms and More* (2011) emphasizes common, yet confusing American sayings that describe real life situations.

P.S. Eric Roth calls Toni "mom."

www.ingramcontent.com/pod-product-compliance
Lightning Source LLC
Chambersburg PA
CBHW062107090426
42741CB00015B/3349